**Theatre
Double Game**

The University of
North Carolina Press
Chapel Hill

Theatre
Double Game

by SAMUEL SELDEN

PN
2039
S4

PREFACE

When I entered the theatre forty-seven years ago—it was the little Provincetown Playhouse run by the triumvirate of Eugene O'Neill, Kenneth Macgowan, and Robert Edmond Jones on MacDougal Street, New York—I fully believed that all drama existed for the sake of the artist—the Actor!—the Dancer!—the Singer!—or the Designer! A few months later, in the middle of winter, I realized my mistake. One morning I found myself in a freezing basement trying to mix a pail of scene paint. The paint was lumpy. Notwithstanding my most earnest effort it was refusing to turn into what it was supposed to be, "a smooth liquid having the consistency of heavy cream." For this action I wore no costume; only a dirty pair of overalls and a sheet of newspaper tied over my hair to protect it from the convulsive "spattering" of the technical director, Cleon Throckmorton. In the middle of the morning an actress, obviously suffering from a cold, entered wrapped in a heavy woolen overcoat. From time to time a harried stage manager crossed and recrossed the basement with an expression fierce enough to have frightened Orpheus out of Hades. The play he was putting together for an opening the following evening was far from ready, and the few but emphatic words he uttered in the breaks of an almost continuous flow of violent sounds, implied the great disappointment he felt in ever having allowed himself to get involved in theatre.

It was there that I began to realize that the "piper who calls the tune" in the playhouse is not the professional performer at all. He is someone else: the person who listens to the performer and responds to his tune—making it, as it were, his own. His theatrical name is "playgoer." At the moment I have just described he was the member of an audience who would sit out front the following night in an attitude of command. The play he would view would in effect be his because he had wished it to exist. He would demand, resolutely *expect*, to be pleased by what was set before him on the stage. If he were to be informed that what he would see had been prepared with great labor and considerable pain, he would reply most certainly, "So what? What conceivably does that have to do with my coming to see your show? I'm interested only in your performance." If after the performance he wished it to discontinue its existence, the play would quickly close up and disappear.

Learning finally that the dominating figure in the theatre is not the play*maker* (though he often likes to think he is), but the play*goer*, I became interested in finding out something about this strange individual with his independent mind. I went to the library. All I could find there were historical notes on the "character" of certain audiences in the time of the Greeks and the Romans, the differences in the "character" of the corresponding groups of people in the Elizabethan period, the Restoration period, and so on, plus an occasional note on specific responses to certain modern plays produced in London, Berlin, Moscow, and such American towns as Ypsilanti, Michigan. But almost nothing at all did I find on *why* the spectators went to the theatre in the first place—these theatres or any theatres.

Through the years since my attachment to the Provincetown I have continued to search the libraries, as well as bookstores and publishers' lists, hoping to catch the appearance of an incisive study of the audience's mind. So far, I have failed to see one. The library shelves across the country are filled with guidebooks for dramatic craftsmanship. They include several manuals on playwriting, many more on acting, a number on directing, and a goodly assortment on designing and general technical practice. Specific aids to scenery construction, painting, costuming, lighting, the making of properties, and the handling of music and sound effects are available in abundance. There are beginning to emerge some useful works on organization and management. Just about all of these look at their subjects strictly from the viewpoint of the stage itself. They discuss their business through the eyes of writers, performers, technicians, and entrepreneurs who already have their minds made up as to what theatre is—or *should* be—and then go on to tell the reader how the validity of their theories can be realized by the application of methods devised by them.

What still seems to me to be singularly lacking is a body of inquiry into the thoughts of the playgoer. He is, after all, the ultimate consumer of the drama for whom the craftsmen labor. It is a commonplace that there would be no theatre without an audience and that the audience cannot be commanded. Maybe the audience *should* come, but if it is not of a mind to come, it simply stays away! The spectator in the playhouse is, as we shall see, a *player*. He wants to play. The function of craftsmen is to work in such a way as to cause the spectator-player to fulfill his desire. But how?

Through forty-seven years I have pursued the answer in many places as an actor, stage manager, technical director, art director, and stage director on and off Broadway, in resident and circuit stock companies (both "one-a-week" and "three-a-week"), in Chautauqua and touring troupes, in a tent-repertory company; then in something over two hundred plays I have directed on the university campuses where I have spent most of my time. The most intensive part of my observation of audiences has been done by watching performances and in reading reports on a dozen outdoor historical plays ("symphonic drama"), by Paul Green, Kermit Hunter, and Robert Emmett McDowell which I have directed, supervised, or advised in North Carolina, Virginia, Kentucky, Illinois, and other states (drawing aggregate attendance through the years of more than three million playgoers). I am referring to this somewhat variegated experience not to accent a personal prowess in craftsmanship, but simply to support the statement that I have had, I think, a rather unusual opportunity to study playgoers' responses.

If I am still in love with audiences, and if I continue to hold a stubbornly optimistic opinion about them, it is not because of any peculiar hardiness in my nature. Rather it is because I have always had a belief in the limitless capacity of the spectator in the playhouse to want and to enjoy well-made dramatic shows. He may not be able to verbalize his wants. At times he will say that he desires something which does not really touch the heart of the hunger that brought him to the auditorium, a hunger for a deeper, wider, more varied experience of living. But this want is there. It is the responsibility of the dramatic artist to find the inward nature of the playgoer's unspoken wish, and to try to satisfy it with all the talent he possesses.

Long ago Shakespeare declared, "one man in his time plays many parts." The final test of the effective theatre man is, I believe, how profoundly he recognizes the impulsion of all of us to play. The greatest game that exists is, of course, the game of life; the second most important is that which is observed where life is vividly recorded, but also extended and resolved in a way not always possible in a daylight experience. It is about the Game of Theatre that this book deals.

Three things I feel should be made clear to the reader before he begins this book. Quite aware that the person we call a playgoer is inevitably an individualist having no fixed behavioral characteristics for the playhouse, I know that it would be futile to try to categorize his thoughts and actions in that house more than very roughly. There are at least a score of distinctively different kinds of audiences, from that kind that craves a drama composed of succulent sugar tits (and even here tastes differ) to that which prefers to pucker its lips on bitter aloes. I am convinced however that away down deep in the soul of every person who ventures into the theatre exist a few common urges that can be identified and that these need to be analyzed.

Second, this book frankly makes no pretense of literary scholarship. The avoidance of the critical attitude is deliberate. It is my purpose here to concentrate on just one aspect that I believe has not yet been sufficiently examined. *Theatre Double Game* keeps its eye from first to last on the playgoer. While he is in the playhouse that part of him which is most responsively alive is not his intellectual faculty (what ponders, refers to, and compares), but that which enters feelingly into the movement, the voice tones, the cries, and the laughter of the figures performing on the stage. The critical exercise does come, but later, after the playgoer has retired from the auditorium to the lobby or has gone home. *Theatre Double Game* deals with the immediate experience—the dance of the senses and what causes it—and how it can be planned by dramatic craftsmen for the enjoyment of the playgoer.

The third point is that *Theatre Double Game* though not labeled a "manual," was designed in fact to be of practical use to playwrights and directors; then, to a lesser degree, to actors and scenic artists. The reader will note that the points for discussion throughout will shift alternately between the stage and the auditorium. It is my hope that also the playgoer wishing to glance at reflections of himself may find here something fresh to think about.

CONTENTS

A State of Playfulness

One man in his time plays many parts.

WILLIAM SHAKESPEARE

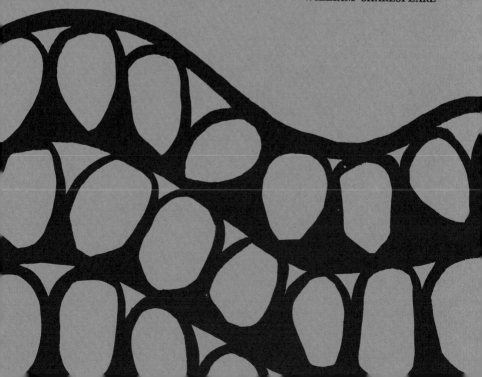

I. THE GAME

and the STAKES

There are many definitions of the Theatre. One describes it as a house where "shows are performed." Another points to dressed-up actors, while still another indicates the crowds of people who gather as spectators to watch a carefully prepared dramatic presentation on a stage. Some of the definitions are quite complicated. The one I have found most evocative is very simple: "a place where an effect is produced on an audience."

This is not the kind of definition that would stand up very well in a book marked for precise terms; however, it comes as close as any statement I have yet seen to catching the essential image of the playhouse. Theatre is a place—it can be round, square or rectilinear, open or closed, and feature a proscenium, thrust, or central stage. It can be big or little, formal or informal, and the spectators who come to it may sit or stand—none of this matters. What is important is that in this place a body of people is moved by what it sees.

What is the act of being moved, one will ask? First, it is something quite voluntary, An audience comes to the place called theatre by its own wish. When it seats itself it knows that the doors through which it made its entrance are unlocked; any spectator can rise freely and depart at any time he desires. He is where he is because he *wants* to be there.

Then what is the sort of experience the prospect of which has persuaded him to come? There are many obvious enticements of course: joining a throng of men and women in a holiday mood, escaping for a little while from a world of dull predictability into another world of pleasant surprises, enjoying bright lights, graceful action, melodious speech and music, and having an opportunity to express one's own feelings with other people's in free unanimity—without having to feel at all self-conscious about it.

Important as is the opportunity that playgoing provides for an act of withdrawal into a state of diversion, it accounts for only a part of the appeal of theatre. Withdrawal is a shift from an actuality. The effect which theatre can and should provide besides is something directly opposite to this; it is a renewed engagement with actual forces, not out of, but in life. In a final analysis this is the more potent, rich, and *moving* element of the theatrical experience.

This second part of the dual effect is difficult to describe neatly. It includes, I believe, three factors which we might call the Sense of Excitement, the Sense of Illumination, and the Sense of Fulfillment. All three are involved in the master sense of a complete existence in which one is exercising by imagination all of one's potentials in body, mind, and spirit. When one feels the stir of a full existence one feels that, using the powers one possesses, one is walking on top of the world instead of being weighted into stillness by the burden of it.

So, the two parts of the effect of theatre are escape and return—but the return is on a different level from the one on which the playgoer started the adventure. The two parts are not antithetical, they are complementary. It is principally with the second part, the return, that I want to deal here.

One premise we must surely accept from the beginning: the attitude of a typical audience is *young*. The playgoer—whatever may be his biological age—is, during the period he is watching a theatrical performance, fundamentally a youthful person. When men and women put themselves in the mood of make-believe, they drop the restrictions imposed on them by adult habits and reach backward toward a condition of childhood. This has been observed so often that it need not be argued here. The spectator in a playhouse opens up his mind to impulse, and on going into the auditorium, deliberately thinks himself young. It may be a condition of precocious childhood— more kin to the adolescent than the toddler—that he assumes. However, whatever it is, it is *young*.

This is especially true about spectators gathered in a group. In such an association they are caught up more freely in the demonstrative than in the deliberative responses of their fellows. Experience has shown that spectators reach to what they see more openly when they are seated close to each other, touching one another, than when they are separated. The physical sense of a slight tremor of excitement, the convulsive movement of a sob, or the softest rumble of a chuckle will provide the trigger for the release of a much fuller expression of feeling. A number of incipient motions or sounds in the darkened auditorium may set off a wave of weeping or a blast of uproarious laughter. The recognition of the youthful inclination of the audience to give vent to its feelings should point up an important clue to why this group of people is where it is.

The best starting point for an investigation of the reason for the spectator's presence is, I am convinced, among the concepts of play. Note the fundamental words of our dramatic vocabulary. People who haunt the theatre are "playgoers." They go to a "playhouse" to see a "play." It is performed by "players." The word "drama" comes from a root word meaning something not read or talked about, but "done." "Theatre," from the Greek *theatron*, was originally a "place for seeing"—a structure where youthful-minded spectators come to observe things acted out— done by actors.

What then is the value of play? There are evocative suggestions in Elmer Mitchell and Bernard Mason's classic treatise, *The Theory of Play*.[1] Human beings *need* to play. "Man," say the authors, "is an active dynamic creature. Activity is the primary need in life." Play is an exercise of function. It is a rehearsal for living. Kittens, puppies, and small children make use of games to enlarge the scope of their learning processes. When little boys and girls run, tumble, bite, assume the roles of bandits and soldiers, manage their dolls, pretend to be doctors or nurses, or to keep house, they are stretching their skills and their horizons. And they are working out methods for holding their own against

1. Elmer D. Mitchell and Bernard A. Mason, *The Theory of Play* (rev. ed.; New York: A. A. Barnes, 1948).

competition. Those young people who have trained themselves in games are apt to think quicker and to act with more perception and assurance than those who have missed this experience.

Later, in those group games we call "sports" the boys and girls discover the more sophisticated qualities of stamina, courage, and loyalty to a group. But they do not cease to have fun. They are "football players," "polo players," "card players," and "chess players."

Play, observes the historian J. Huizinga, is one of the main bases of civilization. Law and order, commerce and profit, craft and art, poetry, wisdom, and science, "all are rooted in the primeval soil of play." Martin Shubick shows, in a book with the elaborate title of *Strategy and Market Structures: Competition, Oligopoly, and the Theory of Games*, how adults as industrial leaders draw on the principles of play they learned as youths in competitive games of football, "prisoners' base," and chess for the plotting of advertising and selling schemes. Generals and lawyers draw on the same kind of early experience for the planning and carrying through of their military campaigns and their court trials. So, often do teachers and preachers and, of course, politicians in their occupations. Move and countermove, strategy and tactics, these are called upon for creating fun when participants are young. Such actions are employed for more serious purposes when people are older. The adult man or woman who never played as a child suffers under a severe disadvantage when he approaches the demands of more complicated social intercourse. Johann Schiller declares in *Aesthetic Letters and Essays*, "Man only plays when in the full meaning of the word he is a man, and *he is only completely a man when he plays*." Huizinga is so firmly convinced of the importance of games in the development of society that he proposes the human creature of the last 2500 years, *Homo Sapiens*, be called also *Homo Ludens*, Playing Man. The book in which he discusses this view at length bears the new term for man as its title.

Play provides then an active, concentrated way of participation in the business of living. It gives one a quickened sense of feeling, thinking, and doing. On occasion it is a substitute. An older dog does not run, he simply makes believe he is running by standing still and barking. The man who has trouble with his sacroiliac or who just does not have time to develop the skill of his throwing arm enjoys sitting in the bleachers at a baseball game and yelling his lungs out over the actions of the hired substitute on the field.

"All that is necessary to explain play," say Mitchell and Mason about man "is the fact that he seeks to live, to use his abilities, to express his personality." If he can't do this directly he does it indirectly. "Make-believe . . . brings compensatory satisfaction, it is a device which compensates for lack of opportunity to express adequately the personality in a cramping environment."[2] In *The Theory of Play and Recreation*, Allen Sapora and Elmer Mitchell suggest, "When new experience and change is denied in actual life, it may be experienced vicariously in theatre. Man in his imagination may defy the inhibitions, fetters and annoyances that envelop him in his world of reality."[3]

But one does not have to be frustrated to enjoy playing. Dr. Eric Berne affirms in *Games People Play* that a person habitually interacts socially with other people by means of games. Unless this interaction is maintained, the person's nervous system figuratively and literally shrivels up. In children's games, both direct and indirect, it is not just the dull or underprivileged children who like to play. Among the active gamesters one finds many bright, full-of-life youngsters. Often they are the most vigorous. Frequently they are the initiators and usually they are the leaders. The same observations can be made about grown people in their general social contacts, and especially about them when they go to the theatre. One attends plays not necessarily because one feels shut in; one may be by nature happy and outgoing. What finally draws a person to a playhouse is something other than just getting an opportunity to *touch* life, it is the

2. *Ibid.*, pp. 81, 94.
3. Allen V. Sapora and Elmer D. Mitchell, *The Theory of Play and Recreation* (3rd ed.; New York: Ronald Press, 1961), p. 150.

prospect of *participating in it more abundantly*. A typical attitude was expressed to me once by a very normal young man:
"Just to be myself in one way through one lifetime is not enough
to satisfy my desire to make the most of my existence on this
earth. I want to be a thousand different people in a thousand
different places in a thousand different times! If I can't do that
really—and I know I can't—I want to exercise my imagination
about it by playing it. That kind of make-believe lessens my
hunger. Besides, it helps me to get a perspective on the one life
I have to lead."

What every normal, red-blooded individual longs for is the
experience of the Good Life. This is an existence in which he
feels he is using for stimulation all his capacities for sensation,
thinking, and feeling, and using them also to obtain a full-bodied
response from his fellows in the most efficient, satisfying way
possible. Those very rare individuals who are convinced that they
are already exercising these powers completely don't have much
use for the theatre. They have just as little use for painting,
music, the dance, and published fiction. The people who still
desire some additional sense of living—even though they may already possess a considerable amount of it—are those who extend
themselves most vigorously in play. The most effective expansive
way they can play is by sensuous imagination, vicariously, in the
theatre.

There are several ways in which one can be affected in a
theatre. Some of them are mild, others are forceful. Not all of
them are truly "dramatic." One way—often undramatic but
nevertheless pleasant—is by just observing. The spectator sits
still for a while watching skilful movements in a dance, or listening to a graceful speech, or to a recital of poetry, or to a program
of songs. A spectator may derive a different, but related, kind
of pleasure by seeing a sketch in which a boy and girl court each
other on a bench in Central Park, or two old colonial officers
reminisce about a military campaign in India long ago. Their
conversation reveals something interesting, perhaps amusing,
about their personalities. Another way—still more different—is

by following from one's seat in the audience a vigorous, lively, but essentially unplotted performance in which a group of actors try to communicate their views on war, politics, the state of human loneliness, or inarticulateness, with a view toward stirring the audience into a certain kind of response. The theme may be anything; the development of it rational or irrational. The purpose is the generating of an emotion through sensuous shock, moments of Dionysian excitement.

Still a third way of being affected in this theatre is by seeing and hearing—and in imagination entering into—an enacted adventure arranged in the form of a story which moves from one point to another. The movement may be rapid or slow, and the influence it exerts on the spectator may be gentle or energetic. The one thing that characteristically distinguishes it from the other two kinds of experience described is that its progress is planned in accordance with a design every part of which is related to the other parts. It has a progress.

These three stage presentations—there are others of course[4]—should be carefully differentiated. When the first kind is arranged as a dramatic work (we are omitting here the completely nondramatic presentations), it has as its aim the displaying of human character caught in a certain mood or direction of movement, interesting to watch without much concern as to how one man influences another man. Foregoing the use of plot, crisis, or suspense, and deliberately freeing itself from any formal beginning or close, it proceeds on an even level and makes its principal appeal on the basis of a colorful and often poetic detail. Examples that come to mind are the impressionistic plays of Maurice Maeterlinck and Eugene O'Neill's more realistic *Moon of the Carribees* and *Bound East for Cardiff*. Among the plays of our modern period is Samuel Beckett's *Krapp's Last Tape*. It is true that the author of this play has something rather pointed, beyond the present scene, to communicate through Krapp's recorded

---

4. Chance Drama, Action Theatre, Total Theatre, New Theatre, Environments, Events, etc., most of them stemming from the concepts of Antonin Artaud and his disciples. See pp. 74–76.

monologue, but the principal appeal this work exerts is as a character vignette. Edward Albee's *The Zoo Story*, in spite of its suddenly active ending, is a character piece.

The second kind of stage presentation is enjoying a strong vogue now. Occasionally sullen, but more often angrily rebellious, it is a development of the concept of the Theatre of Cruelty, promoted by the French author and director Antonin Artaud. It rejects realism, rules of art, and all traditional tenets in an attempt to rediscover the true, the "pure," nature of man's feelings in his barbaric origins. Though it claims to have no regard for old fashioned morality, it often concerns itself vigorously with such subjects as corruption in the federal government, the inequities of the draft laws, and the suffering of the poor. Since the Theatre of Cruelty is determined to throw out all formulas, it turns its back on story form. Although in a feeling respect it stands at the opposite pole from the theatre of poetic mood and character vignette, it bears a resemblance to it in its avoidance of architectonic design. Examples taken from some of the more prominent works at the time of this writing would include Megan Terry's *Viet Rock*, Rochelle Owens' *Futz*, Kenneth Brown's *The Brig*, Jean Genet's *The Blacks* and *The Balcony*, and the prestigious *The Persecution and Assassination of Jean-Paul Marat As Performed by the Inmates of Charenton under the Direction of the Marquis de Sade*, written by Peter Weiss and directed by Peter Brook. There are elements of "cruelty" in Ionesco's *The Lesson*.

The third type of play, and the kind that most properly bears the name of "play," I believe (since it exploits the image of the Game we shall describe in this book), is the plotted work. It makes use of considerable structural paraphernalia to advance story elements. Characteristically it exploits a major conflict, a crisis, and a clear-cut ending. Suspense is the breath of its life. It may be short or long, but whatever its form it holds tenaciously to building its spectator's interest step by step to a climax, the end of the story. *Oedipus* is a plotted play. *Hamlet* is a plotted play. So is *Desire under the Elms* and, in a very quiet but powerful way, *Long Day's Journey into Night. The Glass Menagerie, Death of a Salesman,* and Brecht's *The Good Woman of Setzuan* are plotted plays.

It is not my intention in any way to make a comparison of values between the conventional and the nonconventional—or the "old" and the "new"—because I am convinced that these distinctions have little to do with the ultimate appeal to the spectator. Plotting—the structural arrangement of interrelated scenes marching toward a conclusion—is as new as it is old. Eugene Ionesco began his writing career with plotless stage impressions. They were mostly very short. When he turned to the longer form he employed an inner frame. *Rhinoceros* is a plotted play.

In any case, the form of play we shall deal with principally in this book will be assumed to be a *designed* work; not something created extemporaneously by the actors; not something impulsively "turned on." A work planned, written and rewritten by a playwright, and carefully rehearsed under the direction of a skilled director, with the purpose of satisfying certain basic, long-term desires in the playgoer.

Clearly the principal, the real player in all this activity is the spectator. For convenience in this book I shall call the playgoer also "spectator," "observer," and "member of the audience"—all the same individual. His counterpart on the stage is the "playmaker," frequently called "playcraftsman" and "performer." The actor on the stage is a serious craftsman working as hard as he can to create a good stimulation for play. Sometimes he joins the spectator in having fun; sometimes he has little fun at all, as on those not infrequent nights when he is distracted by illness or worry. At all times he knows that he must drive the show forward so that the sense of play in the playhouse will remain unbroken. Therefore he hides his pain and goes on working. The person who benefits from all of this is, of course, the playgoer. He is the essential make-believer. He employs—actually pays a salary to—the figures who stand, walk, and talk on the stage to instigate in him the spirit of play, and to guide him in the form of that play. The figures of that stage group are then his surrogates, his substitutes in action. By watching them and by projecting himself into their moving and sounding bodies, he enters into that world of fulfilling imagination he came to the playhouse to explore. With the help of the stage group he becomes excited, illumined, and fulfilled through playful activity.

I am heartily in favor of the kind of writing that espouses a "good cause," such as relief for the needy, the end of war, or a more equal justice for minority groups—as vigorous as an author wants to make it—but *not* when this attitude destroys a primary sense of playfulness in the spectator. Emphatically I cannot subscribe to the notion espoused by certain playmakers today that a primary function of a playwright or of an actor is to antagonize the playgoer. To stimulate him, yes. To challenge him, yes. But deliberately to irritate him, no. A normal playgoer is not a masochist; he does not court discomfort, and when he finds it in the playhouse his impulse is to flee from it. The playgoer is quite willing to be persuaded to support a new idea—even a novel, or shocking, one—if he feels he is being led to it playfully, if he senses that he has an active part in the invigorating game of argument and counterargument. And especially if he can do some laughing while he is becoming serious over the new idea.

The playmaker (he may be an actor, a playwright, a director, or a designer) is an artist-specialist. He acts, writes, directs, or plans scenery. But while he fulfills his particular function he does something more than just contribute a discrete part of Effect. He works in close union with his teammates, always in the light of a broad understanding of the total meaning of Play.

An organized play with a number of participants in it is properly arranged into competitive elements. That is, there are the two sides. This is the form of play that is, as we have noted, characteristic of the playhouse. When one asks what exactly are the two sides, the image which immediately springs to mind is of a group of actors lined up behind the footlights and of a mass of spectators on the other side confronting this group. Clearly, from what has been suggested in the foregoing pages, this image is false. The essential confrontation is *in the audience's mind*. The playgoers have come to the playhouse with a desire to find there a way to combat certain undesirable thoughts or feelings (or even a lack of thought or feeling) and they are expecting the craftsman to help them do this. So the play assumes the form of a game of struggle, but a *game stimulated and guided by the playmakers for the playgoer's benefit*.

Here we should attempt, I think, to define the forms of the "game" we are discussing. It is, generally speaking, a competitive activity involving a certain kind of will and endurance between two or more imaginary people engaged in attack and response, so designed as to be especially playfully effective in the environment of a theatre. The spectator, the playgoer, enters by imagination into its life, makes it his own, and is moved by it. This is "the play."

"The play," let us emphasize, constitutes dramatically the principal, the core activity of the playhouse, the kind of activity for which "the playhouse" was named. It is what "the playgoer" impels himself out of his home and crosses town to get engaged in. It is to be *his* experience, *his game*. But he cannot have the pleasure of making himself involved in this game and being moved by it if he does not have the help of trained playcraftsmen. They are the "playmakers." And they too are involved in a kind of game. It is not the same game as that played by the playgoer; the performer is not trying to submerge himself in an imaginative mood. His game is a deliberately practical one; in his success or failure to win this game by craftsmanship lies the extent of his ability to make the principal game, the game the client, the playgoer, wants to play, worth the $1.00 or $10.00 he has paid at the box office for the privilege of participating in it.

The performer, like the imaginary protagonist in the playgoer's play, has an antagonist. "He" is without image—a fact, a condition. "He" is Inertia. So, after all, the performer, like the figure in the play, does have a confrontation. The performer fulfills his function as the initiator of imaginative play and as a guide to the playgoer-as-player by employing a special strategy to overcome the resistance of Inertia. So the Great Game of Theatre viewed in all its dimensions is in fact a double game: a game of imagination played in the mind, the senses, the body of the playgoer, and a game of ministration (for the essential game) played through the body and voice of the performer.

There is no lack of harmony between the two phases of the Great Game. From beginning to end the playcraftsman is working with and for the playgoer. The Inertia which the playmaker exerts himself to combat is a part of the playgoer's nature. But the playgoer claims it unwillingly. As a matter of fact, he employs the playmaker to initiate the play in order to help him rid himself of Inertia. Inertia is the cause of boredom, and boredom is just what the playgoer wishes to have destroyed.

It is to be regretted that we do not have better titles for the two categories of people in the playhouse. If we could designate the "playgoer" (what an insipid word!) by something that meant "play-player," and his stimulator and guide by something like "playmaker and example-giver," our understanding of theatrical relationships would be greatly improved. In this book, we shall examine the way in which the two levels of Theatre Game in the larger sense interact on each other—how the "playgoer" (play-player) and the "performer" (playmaker and guide) work together in imagination and scheme. This should become clear as we go along. For the moment let us return to the level of the playgoer and his play.

The negative forces which the spectator wants to have beaten in the game he is engaged in are those associated with a feeling of life lived incompletely. We might refer to them as boredom (a state of continuous predictability), inertia, blindness, and frustration. The good forces that the spectators would like to have take their places are excitement, illumination, and fulfillment. The first are dark, the second light. The first are devils, the second angels. The game that is set up in the theatre lines up the opponents in this way:

Positive	vs.	Negative
Excitement		Inertia
Illumination		Blindness
Fulfillment		Frustration

Though most of the best of the dramatic games employ all six of these forces, some of them do not. It is safe to affirm, I think, that all successful plays—that is, all really *effective*, dramatic plays—do include the first two, at least: excitement *vs.* inertia. Some plays exploit the opposition between these first forces in order to emphasize a conflict between illumination and blindness, while others (many of them) use the excitement *vs.* inertia combat in order to highlight a fight between fulfillment and frustration. Dr. Berne points out in *Games People Play* that what is struggled for by all people seeking to achieve a fuller, more satisfactory use of their human functions in social contacts are (1) an exercise of their body (chiefly their senses); (2) an exercise of their minds (in understanding and planning); and (3) a movement toward a goal. These correspond to the three desires of the spectator we have just noted: excitement, illumination, and fulfillment.

Pointing to positive and negative forces and trying to relate them to a spectator's ceaseless desire to expand the limits of his human existence may seem to suggest that I regard the theatre as being a kind of sanatorium to which sick or weak people go for therapy. This is not my intention. The playhouse should always be the home of wonder, of playfulness for eminently healthy, *growing* people. But it must be more than an institution dedicated only to tickling the exterior senses of its devotees. As J. L. Styan has put it simply: "We go to the theatre as one of the means by which we come to terms with life."

The following chapters of this book will attempt to describe in as concrete terms as possible what I believe I have found out about the natures and forms of the "good" and "bad" forces of drama, in a search in which I have been engaged for nearly half a century. The search has gone on in many different places and, on my part, in many different capacities—as an actor, a technician, a scenic artist, primarily as a director, and, of course, as a spectator. I have interviewed playgoers, I have talked with critics; mostly I have watched and listened to audiences.

I will start with the prime element of *excitement*.

Being Alive

Energy is eternal delight.
WILLIAM BLAKE

II. *A Sense of Excitement—*
CHANGE

There are some feelings that are very hard to put into words. One of them, strangely enough, is that which one experiences on going to the theatre. Among the many people I have interviewed about a session of spectating, very few could state clearly what they had felt. They would speak warmly about details, it is true— an actor's interpretation of his role, the two-minute scene between a child and its mother at the head of the stairs, the leading lady's costumes, or the quality of the moonlight that shone through the bedroom window. But about what *in general* it was that had attracted them to go to this play in this theatre this evening, and how *in general* they had liked what they saw, this they had difficulty in expressing.

For the negative side of a playgoer's feelings the words appear to come rather freely. He can tell you quite pointedly what he is trying to escape. The business man will speak about that long week his rebellious nose was pressed to the grindstone, his wife about the new year's housecleaning and the sickness of her children, the clerk about her tired feet at the store, and the typist about all those month-end bill forms at the office. One student told me quite frankly that he was attending a play I had directed because he had flunked his French; another stated that he was trying to forget that his best girl would not be at the midwinter dance. Seventy charming, lively young ladies from a neighboring boarding school all declared on a questionnaire that they had come to our production for one reason only: "To get away from St. Mary's!" I cannot say that I felt very much complimented by any of these confessions. Still, I tried to derive some satisfaction from the knowledge that we had given a number of good people a momentary freedom from their woes whatever they were!

On the positive side, the question, "Why do you go to the theatre?" elicits favorable responses that make no mention at all of escape. The answer is usually phrased in just two words, "for entertainment." This is not very illuminating, of course, since "entertainment" stands for so many different things that it creates no clear image of anything. However, by associating the term "entertainment" with all the impressions reported about a show recently seen, one perceives that what the word finally means is "stimulation." A simpler word is "excitement." Fundamentally, everyone goes to the playhouse to be stirred, to become excited!

This is surely not a very profound observation. The search for the cause of the playgoer's fascination in theatre has to go a step further. It has to find what is at the heart of a certain kind of excitement that makes that excitement dramatic. It has its roots, I think, in a sensitive and balanced perception of contrasts.

The most debilitating kind of pain that can be experienced by any human being is boredom. Each of us is so constructed as an organism that we can have no awareness of ourselves as a living thing at all except as we *sense* our surroundings. When we within ourselves cannot have the full awareness of a reaction to something outside of ourselves we feel strangled. Stimulus-hunger is similar to food-hunger but it causes greater agony. The infant who is denied handling by a parent degenerates very quickly, and unless the experience is reversed in time the child is likely to grow up into a physical and mental cripple. He may die. Grown people deprived of a large amount of sensuous stirring-up are usually sickly. Experiments in the laboratory have shown that simple electric shocks have frequently restored unhealthy animals to strength just because their nerves were titillated.

There is no question of course about certain kinds of stimuli being more pleasurable than others. The most important thing to recognize however is that there must be *some* stimulation. What gives a certain stimulus its special pointedness is the fact that we, the senser, are aware of its difference from another.

"Variety is the spice of life." How often have we heard this. I am certain that the commonplace is true. But only in part. The full truth is that variety is more than the spice, it comes close to being the whole dish.

If one wants to see the real meaning of variety one has only to consider what human existence would be without it. What strange kind of life would a man lead if it had no contrasts in it, if, for instance, he could perceive no variation between light and dark, or between warm and cold? What would people experience if there were no ups and downs, no youth and age, no male and female, no peace and turmoil, or none of the thousands of other sensations and conditions between which men now make comparisons? In its very simplest terms, life depends on breathing, and that consists of two contrary motions: inhaling and exhaling.

Pointed changes of nature are inherently dramatic. Sunrise after night, sundown after daylight, a clear morning after rain, the first cold autumn wind after a warm summer—these are breath-taking when they are observed freshly. The sense of surprise, the sense of wonder, is what makes their effect. A heavy fall of snow in Butte, Montana, may occur almost without comment, while just a light flurry of flakes in Los Angeles will cause so much excitement that the schools will have to close.

The anthropologists tell us that the most alert individuals tend to be those who inhabit the geographical zones where there is a strongly marked rotation of the seasons. Neither continuous winter nor continuous summer is conducive to human brightness. It is a curious fact that peoples who inhabit places unvarying in climate seem to lack a sense of history. Perhaps this is because they find it difficult there to attach their communal memories to varying images of ice and wind, or rain, or sunshine, and to the spurts or relaxation of endeavor which these changes stimulate. The restless disposition of the inhabitants of such strange areas as Southern California where the weather seems always to be stuck in spring is caused by a peculiar condition which compensates for a lack of seasonal change. The temperature fluctuates widely within each period of twenty-four hours. So, by way of equivalence, the human organism in California is subjected, in an abbreviated way, to the effects of what would be caused elsewhere by a yearly shift.

Some of the physical scientists plumbing the heart of the atom and its mirrored image in the antiatom have arrived at a theory that there may exist, unseen and unheard but still perceptible by us, a whole great anti-universe, an opposite of the one we feel more naturally about us. If the existence of this other reverse macrocosm can be verified, the concepts of the human creatures can be stretched in a staggering way. Are you and I, seen and heard as two people, actually four people, each of us composed of opposite minds, opposite feelings, opposite souls? Maybe each thought we think is a contradiction. Who knows? Quite possibly it is this inherent oppositeness of each of us which makes the oppositeness of sentient experience between two people so stimulating to us.

Fortunately, our search for dramatic effect does not have to wait for the solution of universal forms; we can find the nature of it in very simple everyday sensations. I recall a lazy summer afternoon in Santa Monica, California, where I was sitting with our Irish setter, Lady, in the garden enjoying the sun and trying to read a rather dull magazine. The setter was lying half asleep on the grass. What made her drowsy was not a surrounding condition of stillness—a noisy group of children were romping nearby, and cars and trucks were passing along a street within a stone's throw of where she lay. Rather, it was the lasting feeling of *sameness*. Then, the figure of a moving cat caught the corner of Lady's vision. She suddenly became alert. She lifted her head, she jumped to her feet and started to bark. The dog had become aware of something *different*, and that awareness was causing a tension in every muscle of her body.

I was roused by the passing incident of the cat but immediately after it returned to my languid reading. Since it was a warm day and I had nowhere I wanted to go I was wearing a pair of open sandals. I had scarcely noticed the cat. I was no longer thinking of it. I was not much stirred by my reading. I was quite relaxed. Then an ant crawled over one of my bare toes. It got my complete attention. I was disturbed by it. First, I tried to brush the tiny animal with my fingers; failing to dislodge it I jumped to my feet and shook the ant off with a vigorous kick. All of this action was caused by a faint tickle of a body almost too small to see—simply because it had caused a *novel* sensation.

I remember also with amusement the evidence of an early morning torment suffered by a writer who moved from Brooklyn to a North Carolina town. He had come to expect the recurrent roar of passing elevated trains so much that it never affected his sleep. In the country town he became dark-eyed just because he was awakened by the unexpected song of a mockingbird!

The incidents involving the cat, the ant, and the mockingbird were dramatic—in a miniature but effective way, exciting—because each of them embraced an opposite. But it was not just the existence of the opposites that caused an effect, it was the *shift* from one to the other. Each shift called for a marked and quick adjustment for which the body experiencing the shift was not at that moment prepared. It was taken by surprise.

So the key word for excitement is *change*. The illustrations give point to a very simple definition of dramatic effect. It is *a feeling of excitement, generated in someone by the shock of a sudden and forceful change*. The shock is theatrically stirring if the elements contrasted are strongly indicated, if the pressure for an adjustment between them is marked, and if the alteration of condition caused by this crisis in which they are involved with each other is clear and quick.

One of the sharpest illustrations of theatrical change (on a big scale) I remember is a moment in the outdoor, "symphonic" play, *The Lost Colony* by Paul Green, which I directed annually for twelve years on Roanoke Island, North Carolina. The drama concerns the initial English settlement that included women and children in the New World. The scene is the chapel in a log fort and the time is a quiet, sunny afternoon. The priest has just entered the chapel with a group of the colonists to give thanks to God for the safe delivery of the baby, Virginia Dare. The men and women, filling the stage, are kneeling reverently. Father Martin stands by the altar above them with his arms lifted in gratitude to God—when suddenly there is a yell from a sentinel:

"Indians! They're killing Master Dare!" A blunderbuss is discharged, the women scream, and the men rush for their guns.

What makes this moment particularly effective in my memory is that all at once there is a change from a mood of prayerful thanksgiving to one of noisy horror. And then, on top of this, is still another change, more profound than the sensory shift. Captain Dare is the father of Virginia. At the same time he is a leader of the effort to wrest this wilderness from hostile elements and to tame it. What should be for him a moment of supreme joy—for a kind of victory in life—becomes instead the moment of his defeat in death.

I like to remember by way of comparison with this epic shift a much more intimate but equally pointed change in Lillian Hellman's *The Little Foxes*. It occurs in the scene where Horace Giddens, suffering from a critical heart ailment and just brought back from the hospital, sits in a wheel chair in the sitting room of his home. Regina, his wife, is across the table from him. She has been telling him slowly how she has never loved him. As she continues, he puts his hand to his throat. Regina informs him that she knows he will die, and she will be lucky. Horace reaches tremblingly for a bottle of medicine, but drops it and spills its contents. Gasping, he asks his wife to call the maid to get the other bottle upstairs. She does not move. In her cold eyes he sees that the end has come. Life and death, another violent change. The spectator following this, senses the sting of it in his own body.

At precisely the time when Oedipus is most eager to find the cause of the plague in Thebes he discovers that he himself is the object he has been searching. Portia has just been hailed by Shylock as a "Daniel come to judgment" when she turns the case against him by stating that he may take a pound of Antonio's flesh but not one jot of blood. Nora in *A Doll's House* is in a most disadvantageous position—playing with her children under a table—when Krogstad, the one man whom she least wants to see, comes into the room to speak to her. The Master Builder has climbed triumphantly to the top of the scaffolding of his new house when his foot slips and he falls to his death. In *The Devil's Disciple*, the British soldiers hunting for the Reverend Anderson, see Dick Dudgeon, the most unsaintly person in the village, in the minister's coat and seize him, thinking they have their man. At that point when the lonely Laura in *The Glass Menagerie* feels that she may at last have made a conquest, the gentleman caller informs her that he is engaged to another girl. Biff, the beloved son of Willy Loman in *Death of a Salesman*, takes a trip to see his father, and walks in on him right at the time he is entertaining a prostitute. The long-awaited Orator of Ionesco's *The Chairs* steps up on the speaker's platform and reveals that he is a deaf mute. The outcast Jerry in Albee's *The Zoo Story* induces a stranger in the park to draw a knife, and impales himself on it.

The device of juxtaposing two opposites, one expected and one unexpected, and thus forcing the spectator to make a quick adjustment in his senses and his mind between the two has been used as frequently in comedy as in serious drama. The male lovers in *A Midsummer Night's Dream*, wrongly anointed by Puck's elixir suddenly begin chasing the wrong women. Old Bottom makes a startling appearance in an ass's head. Viola dressed as a boy and carrying a greeting of affection from the Duke Orsino to the Lady Olivia, is shaken when she realizes that she is the object of Olivia's love. The disillusioned Orgon emerges from his hiding place under the table to unmask the imposter Tartuffe. The shy young Marlowe in *She Stoops to Conquer* is chagrined when he suddenly finds out that the pretty serving maid he has been wooing in a rather free and easy way is the well-born daughter of one of his father's most respected friends. Modern plays like Thornton Wilder's *The Matchmaker* are full of such comic surprises. These and the foregoing more serious situations are obvious examples of that kind of shock which touches the nerve of the observer. Between and around such high incidents in every successful play are of course many smaller, slighter, changes of action, sensation, and thought which fill out the body of the theatrical motion.

The opposing parties in a dramatic interaction need not be

two or more people; they may be just two sides ("good" and "bad," "strong" and "weak") within a single character, such as Hamlet; or a man and a force of nature, such as the old man and the sea in O'Neill's *Anna Christie*. Often the interaction is an exchange between a whole group of people and an opposing force with which the group contends. In Karel Capek's play about the automatons called "robots," the engineers who made them have recently learned of a revolt. Barricaded in the sitting room of their superintendent's home on an isolated island, the little band of survivors huddle around an electric lamp. The current that feeds this light comes from a distant dynamo tended by other human beings. Of this, the engineers are aware. So long as the light burns the engineers know that they are not alone; the light symbolizes for them the promise of their continuing existence. They talk about it; the more they regard it the more hopeful they become. They speak to each other about their dreams for the future. At the very height of this wishful talk there is an explosion. The lamp flickers and goes out; the men become silent. The implication is clear; the race of man is doomed.

One of the surest ways of arriving at a comic feeling is to get oneself into a state of guessing—having to adjust oneself time and again in spite of every effort not to be caught being wrong. Consider *The Comedy of Errors* with its two Dromios. As twins they are, in a way, one, yet by inclination each wants to establish his separate identity. So, they are very much opposites in spirit. Throughout the play until the ending they are taken repeatedly for each other, being given gifts and messages and told to go on errands totally inappropriate under the circumstances. Each twin is in effect fighting with his shadow. The shifts from expectation to disillusionment caused by this continual forced transference of their individualities instills in each a feeling of outrage. The spectator plays a game of trying to keep up with all of the changes. Finding how difficult it is he appreciates the justification for the comic displays of desperation and is impelled to laugh over them.

The spectator, playing the game of theatre by putting himself into certain attitudes of mind then suddenly reversing them, finds that change is, in a playful way, wonderfully stimulating. What this amounts to is teasing himself with tensions. Someone has remarked that the most pleasurable thing in life is the experience of relaxation after a state of nervous stress. In the theatre a man can make himself have a feeling of release over and over again. He can have a sense of momentary freedom in everyday life, of course, but he cannot count on it; often he finds himself in a condition of tightness from which he cannot extricate himself at all. Or, if he finally does extricate himself, the effort has taken so long that he has missed entirely the rush of that sense of well-being that comes from a *quick* untying of the knot. In the presence of a reputable work of art the spectator knows that he will not be left in his tensions, and that the relaxation will be so devised as to give him a maximum satisfaction.

So far in this chapter we have been looking at theatre game through the eyes of the playgoer or play-player (see p. 14) as he feels out sensuously the interactions between contrasting forces provided for his attention on the stage, so attaining a state of excitement. Now we will turn to the playmaker, the craftsman, to see how he devises ways for leading the playgoer into the kind of experience of tension and release he wants to have.

The feeling of change is centered in the variation of attitudes. Since change makes the playgoer pleasurably excited he likes to have a dramatic performance titillate his sentient capabilities on every possible level. Therefore, the able craftsman works for variation from the bottom of his stage creation to the top of it. First, he appeals to plain sensuous responsiveness. While the world outside is drab, the playhouse's interior is colorful. While the street is noisy, the auditorium is hushed. While the illumination of the city is frankly utilitarian, the lights of the theatre induce a mood. They create an expectation of a heightened excitement to come. The curtain is down, then it goes up—and a wholly new experience begins to unfold.

Good dialogue is not just a string of words. It is a pattern of rapid verbal exchanges. The form of this interplay between two people talking is like that of a tennis ball stroked back and forth between two sportsmen. No one observing the play can tell before the ball goes over the net just where it will strike or just how it will be returned. It may be lobbed; it may be directed straight to one's opponent's racket. This progress of the ball from court to court is a series of surprises.

Here is a fragment of a conversation between Viola and Olivia in *Twelfth Night*.

VIOLA. Are you the lady of the house?

OLIVIA. If I do not usurp myself, I am.

VIOLA. Most certain, if you are she, you do usurp yourself; for what is yours to bestow is not yours to reserve. But this is from my commission. I will on with my speech in your praise, then show you the heart of my message.

OLIVIA. Come to what is important in it. I forgive you the praise.

VIOLA. Alas I took great pains to study it, and 'tis poetical!

OLIVIA. It is more like to be feigned. I pray you keep it in. I heard you were saucy at my gates, and allowed your approach rather to wonder at you than to hear you.

Bouncing dialogue is characteristic of comedy. It appears just as appropriately in serious plays. Here are the opening speeches in *Hamlet*:

BERNARDO. Who's there?

FRANCISCO. Nay, answer me: stand and unfold yourself.

BERNARDO. Long live the king!

FRANCISCO. Bernardo?

BERNARDO. He.

FRANCISCO. You come most carefully upon your hour.

BERNARDO. 'Tis now struck twelve; get thee to bed, Francisco.

FRANCISCO. For this relief much thanks: 'tis bitter cold, And I am sick at heart.

BERNARDO. Have you had quiet guard?

FRANCISCO. Not a mouse stirring.

BERNARDO. Well, good night.

But before Francisco can leave two other figures enter and the path of the conversation ceases to resemble that of a tennis ball in a singles match. We are now listening to the strokes of a doubles match. Not every passage of dialogue has exactly the character of a tennis game, of course. There are long sections of speaking in *Hamlet* in which the ball moves back and forth more deliberately and thus makes one think of football, perhaps. Other comic and serious scenes resemble basketball, baseball, or even polo matches.

If one should wish to compare the dialogue of a Shakespearean comedy with that of a different, modern work, one could not pick anything much more opposite than Samuel Beckett's *Waiting for Godot*. Beckett happens to be an avowed anti-theatricalist. His strong distaste for any form of dramatic formula writing does not, however, apply to the use of small-scale changes.

VLADIMIR. Charming evening we're having.
ESTRAGON. Unforgettable.
VLADIMIR. And its not over.
ESTRAGON. Apparently not.
VLADIMIR. It's only the beginning.
ESTRAGON. It's awful.
VLADIMIR. It's worse than being at the theatre.
ESTRAGON. The circus.
VLADIMIR. The music hall.[1]

This passage resembles the rapid strokes in a rally. The essential bounce remains in the more leisurely series of interchanges.

(*Silence. Vladimir deep in thought, Estragon pulling on his toes.*)
VLADIMIR. One of the thieves was saved.
    (Pause.)
It's a reasonable percentage.

1. Samuel Beckett, *Waiting for Godot* (New York: Grove Press, 1954), p. 23.

(Pause.)
Gogo.
ESTRAGON. What?
VLADIMIR. Suppose we repented.
ESTRAGON. Repented what?
VLADIMIR. Oh . . .
    (*He reflects.*)
We wouldn't have to go into details.
ESTRAGON. Our being born?
    (*Vladimir breaks into a hearty laugh which he immediately stifles, his hand pressed to his pubis, his face contorted.*)
VLADIMIR. One daren't even laugh any more.
ESTRAGON. Dreadful privation.
VLADIMIR. Merely smile.
    (*He smiles suddenly from ear to ear, keeps smiling, ceases as suddenly.*)
It is not the same thing. Nothing to be done.
    (*Pause.*)
Gogo.
ESTRAGON. (*Irritably.*)
What is it?
VLADIMIR. Did you ever read the Bible?
ESTRAGON. The Bible . . .
    (*He reflects.*)
I must have taken a look at it.
VLADIMIR. Do you remember the Gospels?
ESTRAGON. I remember the maps of the Holy Land. Coloured they were. Very pretty. The Dead Sea was pale blue. The very look of it made me thirsty. That's where we'll go, I used to say, that's where we'll go for our honeymoon. We'll swim. We'll be happy.
VLADIMIR. You should have been a poet.[2]

Beckett verifies his interest in the bouncing pattern of dialogue when a little later he has Vladimir appeal to Estragon:

2. *Ibid.*, pp. 8-9.

"Come on, Gogo, return the ball," and makes his companion reply with exaggerated interest, "I find this really most extraordinarily interesting."

The major dramatic changes begin in the phase of characterization. In various aspects of Hamlet he contrasts himself in turn with Claudius, with his mother, with Polonius, with Ophelia, with the Ghost. For the sake of a central series of confrontations in the drama Shakespeare makes him seem most opposite of all to the King. From a second point of view Hamlet is presented as a contrast in himself. He is an intellectual trying to be a man of action; and in the light of this struggle his dominant personality alters between the beginning and the end of the story. As one human image replaces another—immediately or a little more deliberately—in the spotlight, the spectator has to readjust his responsive frame of mind and thus the game of interchange goes on; one figure plays against another, then the other plays against him. A little later perhaps they band together against a third figure. And so on.

If one turns once more from Shakespeare to Beckett, one notes immediately the contrasting differences between the imaginative and better educated Vladimir, and the realistic Estragon who thinks, talks, and acts with greater directness. Pozzo and Lucky are similarly contrasted. Regarded as teams, Vladimir and Estragon are opposed to Pozzo and Lucky. The Boy is unlike any of the others. As the focus in dialogue moves from one individual to another, the attentive response of the playgoer has each time to make an adjustment, and that experience contributes, moment by moment, to his alertness. For him, the "ball" of speech continues to bounce itself through his mind.

One of the most obvious aspects of change is in the moods of scenes. The drama of Hamlet begins on the ramparts of the castle in the bitter cold, with a group of soldiers talking excitedly about a disembodied spirit. At the close of this bit of rapid conversation we are transported to the ponderous courtroom where a stuffed king talks heavily to a bored prince. As soon as Claudius and the Queen make their slow exit, the prince's friends rush in to tell him about the ghost. To contrast with this bit of nervous excitement, the playwright transports our attention to Polonius and his platitudes, then back to the crisis outside the castle. Thus, the action progresses. No two succeeding scenes are alike in feeling.

In *Godot* the changes of mood are generally more subtle. There are fairly strong changes, however, at those points where Pozzo and Lucky intrude themselves into the scene. There is a difference between the impacts of their two appearances, caused by a reversal of their relationship between their first and second entrances. Another quieter sequence of mood variations is effected by the changes of topic in the dialogue. Vladimir and Estragon discuss the experience of sleeping in a ditch, then Estragon's old shoes, then the two thieves at the Crucifixion, the dead tree under which they are standing, Godot's failure to appear, the beginning of a bawdy story, the smell of garlic, and a question about hanging. Beckett is a master of that sort of conversation which jumps from subject to subject, yet keeps intact a certain sense of connectedness.

Where Shakespeare and Beckett part company most forcibly is in the supreme aspect of change, that involving the contours of plot. Shakespeare and nearly all of the traditional dramatists both ancient and modern insist on leading the attention and the feelings of the playgoer up and down (or down and up) and often also in and out. This serves as a natural reflection, intensified a little, of the playgoer's yen for change. Shakespeare's dramas are constructed around a scheme of shifting tensions building to a climax. So are the works of nearly all the leading authors since his time. Beckett has inserted no plot form in *Godot*; the end of the association of the two men we are observing is no different from the beginning. The author has given us enough variation in the smaller appeals to our attentions to hold us interested for an hour. Two hours of *Waiting for Godot*, however, would be intolerable.

Here is a problem that I have had to contend with in my university playwriting courses. Those who object to running the expectation of the spectator up and down and working on his feelings of suspense and fulfillment like to argue that it is a throwback to the age of stale Romanticism to want to have a story. My reply is that when one omits plot from a dramatic design one is taking away one of the most potent factors of dramatic effect—change.

Apprentice dramatists will point to certain of the newer compositions which do appear to hold the spectator's attention very well without plot—but only for a short period of time. I have noted that the limit of time is usually about twenty minutes. (Beckett, a master of variable dialogue, is able to do little better than this.) That represents the period in which novelty of setting, subject matter, character, or dialogue remains effective for the playgoer. Beyond that, the attentiveness of the audience inevitably wears off. The playgoer's urge to have his life in the playhouse moved by change is not dependent in any way on tradition or fashion. It is a fundamental part of his unalterable human nature.

One objection one hears to including the larger twists and turns of a plot among the factors of dramatic effect is that the changes which make up its characteristic form are not sudden, often not even swift. Early in *Hamlet*, the Prince is convinced that Claudius has killed his father and should be punished, yet it is not until near the end of the fifth act that he shows enough courage to put a rapier into the King's body. At the beginning of *A Doll's House*, Nora is a child wife. Not until the very end of a long sequence of events does she reveal her altered character to the playgoer by slamming the door on her husband's house. Willy Loman in *Death of a Salesman* has to go through many scenes of depression, then optimism, then depression, then optimism again before he makes his decision to kill himself by crashing his car. Can the larger bumps and valleys in these stories be regarded as occurring sufficiently swiftly, sufficiently shockingly, to make them dramatic to the spectator?

Yes, emphatically, I believe they can. What must be recognized always is that what counts is not the actual measure of time but the mental and emotional impression of time made on the playgoer. In the world of reality outside the playhouse the series of actions which lead up to the final altered condition of a Hamlet, a Nora, or a Willy Loman might extend over a period of months or years, and the last great shift might occur so quietly that no one observing it would feel very much stirred by it. On the stage, however, all this is compressed into a period of just two hours. The edges of the critical events are sharpened with respect to each other and the significance of the big moment at the end is underlined. Thus the total effect becomes striking. The wrench of personal adjustment to the shocks that occur during a short two-hours' time is what makes the playgoer pleasurably aware of dramatic effect.

So, the pattern for excitement through change includes small turns, intermediate turns, and big turns. Sensuous, physical, or psychological, each makes its own peculiar contribution to catching and maintaining the attention of the playgoer and driving along his feeling of engagement in what is happening on the stage—from 8:30 right through the evening till the curtain falls at 10:45.

In this first chapter about excitement we have given considerable space to mental factors in dramatic change. If we wished to show a stricter parallel between our three divisions of a playgoer's desire and Dr. Berne's grouping of physical exercise plus mental exercise plus the pursuit of a goal in people's playing (see p. 15), we should have sharpened the emphasis in this chapter perhaps on the purely bodily responses. The dramatic game at its best is always very physical. But it is bound to be at the same time, partly mental; in the integrated human organism somatic and psychic are closely bound together. The factor we have tried most especially to underline here however is the *alertness of the senses*. Since the recognition and enjoyment of change almost inevitably involves challenges to eyes, ears, nose, fingers, and taste buds before there can be a jump in the mind, the experiences of change belongs very much in the first category of playgoers' desires. The player in the theatre seat bases all other experiences in the playhouse on what changes his senses are telling him to notice.

What makes a complete experience of dramatic change includes not one, but three basic steps. The first is anticipation, a suspenseful forecasting of a shift of equilibrium coming; second, the crisis or actual turn; and third, an emotional looking-back on the turn. Hamlet in the Players Scene creates a sense of excitement in the spectator by his baiting of the "mouse trap" for Claudius; still more when he forces the King to reveal himself (this is the principal twist); and some development of the same feeling in his comment to Horatio after the King's departure.

The more extended the implications involved in the disturbance wrought by a change—implications concerning other disturbances in the past and probable disturbances in the future—the more profound is the emotional response of the spectator toward the particular change he is contemplating. In other words, the contrasting conditions between which the change takes place must be related in the mind of the spectator if the effect of the change on him is to be dramatic rather than merely surprising or shocking. This is just another way of stating the old principle of form that has been applied for centuries to all the arts: "Contrast within the framework of Unity." In art as in life the human organism craves change, but change held together by a continuity of experience.

III. *A Sense of Excitement*

—ACTION

In my search for what causes that state of feeling we call "dramatic excitement" I believe I have discovered three stimulants. The first is change. The second is action. The third is feeling and we will deal with it in the next chapter. Change and action are closely related, as I shall attempt to show.

Action, like change, produces an invigorating effect on the playgoer, not because it is a dramatic device especially applicable to theatrical experience, but because it is an expression of natural impulse in or out of the playhouse. Human existence would be intolerable without action. For thousands of years man has run and jumped, and hurled hammers and javelins against the records of other men. He has danced, swum, dived from high places, and swung from trapezes. When he could not make his own body reach the physical goals he longed for, he has mounted animals and ridden machines. From the beginning man has beggared himself for fast horses, then even faster cars and still faster airplanes. Now he craves to mount rockets. If he cannot do it himself, he insists on the right to see the movement of others through a television eye.

Movement as movement, however, is stimulating relatively. Whether it is experienced directly in oneself or indirectly through another body, it is sensuously exciting only as it comes newly to a person's awareness. Movement long continued even in imagination loses its stirring quality; it may even make one languorous. In the future when vehicles travel to the moon at the speed of thousands of miles an hour, passengers will hold their breaths at take-off then, after an hour or two in flight, yawn and take a nap, only to become alert once more when they approach the landing. Finally, what causes the effect we call a sense of action is not so much the movement itself as the feeling of a *change* from another condition.

An alteration from movement to stillness can be arresting.

Nevertheless, the reverse is usually more impressive because potentially, at least, it makes greater demands on the faculties of adjustment in the individual responding. Proof of this is in the different reaction a "talky" play gets from that produced by an "active" one. No dramatist that I am aware of has ever been able to compose a successful stage piece in which two characters remained seated throughout just speaking into each other's eyes.

Under certain circumstances the alerting influence—the influence which sets the responding organism into an attitude of action—is not a bodily shifting, but something else. Who has not "popped out of his skin" at the sudden ringing of a telephone? The slamming of a door or even the sudden calling of his name will often make a person start. He is most likely to do this if the sound is connected by feeling with something he dreads— or hopes for. The little boy in the process of stealing cookies in the pantry will be put into a state of active alertness simply by the sound of a footfall outside the door. A girl expecting a caller may assume an attitude of nervous excitement for no other reason than that she has heard the faint creaking of a screen door.

Action and the disturbance of an equilibrium then are two sides of the same coin. The individual who experiences the new tension has a feeling of action. This person may be the central player in a drama of life, or he may be just an observer, such as the spectator in a theatre who sympathetically follows the stage person's dramatic adventure. What Desdemona does as she struggles to free herself from the choking hands of Othello is felt by everybody in the audience.

The need for action in the theatre is so clear that it never gets any argument from either craftsmen or critics. Everyone will say easily, "Yes, of course we must have action here!" Confusion starts however when one is asked to define the term. What *is* action really? Nine out of ten persons will answer simply, "movement." From a dramatic point of view this is, as we have just noted, a very poor definition. When someone attempts to describe action this way to me I think immediately about my home in Santa Monica (in the days when the whole family lived there), and all the movement which occupied it but attracted very little attention. The mother of the family walks back and forth in the kitchen getting dishes and pans, shifting kettles on the stove, dishing up meals, and carrying the food to the dining table. The father leaves the house in the morning and steps back into it in the evening. He sits in a chair and turns the pages of his newspaper. The girl of the family goes up the stairs to take off her coat. The boy stoops down to tie his shoelace. Through twenty-four hours of the day the clocks in the house move their hands around and around. Periodically the motor in the refrigerator runs to adjust the temperature. This is movement. But is it action? No, since nobody pays any particular attention it cannot be—in a dramatic sense—action. Before the end of the evening, perhaps, some member of the family will remark, "I wish something would happen!"

Now, what will one say if there is a sudden change of tempo? Mother drops a hot dish on the floor of the kitchen, Father enters the front door swearing, the girl on her way upstairs inexplicably bursts into tears, her brother catches a shoelace on a step and falls off a ladder. A clock or the refrigerator motor unexpectedly emits a whirring sound. These cannot help but attract attention. An element of difference has been added to motion. This is the new element of perceptible change.

Let us repeat, it is quite possible, on occasion, to have action without physical motion at all. The simplest illustration of this is a caution light on a highway. At a certain kind of intersection there may be a double blinker composed of two amber lights placed next to each other. First one flashes, then the other, back and forth. In a way, this signal gives the effect of motion; the eye of the driver must snap from one light to the other and back again. At another intersection, however, there will be a single blinker. Through space, this light goes nowhere, it only flashes. It is on then off; on, then off; that is all. Yet it creates the sense of motion. What makes this sense is *change*.

Thus, action and change are unified. They are essentially two aspects of the same phenomenon. A single alteration, a unit of change, becomes "action" when it is perceived to be a part of a series. "Action" doesn't stop, it goes on. When Mother drops the dish, Father runs into the kitchen to help her; when Father comes in the front door swearing, his family wants to know what it is all about. These units of activity lead to others. Later in the evening when the group looks back on all that has happened it will remark, "What a hectic couple of hours these have been!"

The most powerful agent for a continuity of action is, of course, a human drive toward a goal. Something must be attained or something must be preserved. As long as the effort at adjustment is still in progress the feeling of action is alive. The great drives take time to get satisfied—or defeated. The skillful playwright, helped by his actors and the director, will take a whole performance to work out a solution to one of them. During all of this time the spectator will feel the presence of action.

If the thing desired, the goal to be reached, can be realized easily, there are not likely to be any sharp changes of condition along the way which will make for dramatic effect. So there will be no genuine sense of action. The situation will be different if the adventurous search for achievement is attended by difficulties. The more intense the difficulties, and the more unrelenting their pressure on the individual's striving, the stronger must be the exercise of a man's will. Consequently, the more compelling tends to be the whole process of pushing toward the goal.

Difficulties can simply put a stop to striving. Then, there ceases to be any activity. However, the difficulties may be overcome. If they are overcome quickly there is no extended action. If, after Hamlet's first confrontation with the King following the revelation of the Ghost, the King should cave in, admit his guilt, and abdicate his throne, there would be no more drama in the play. Excitement occurs only when the pressure between resistance and will is maintained over a period of time. Therefore, the most effective factor for a dramatic action is a conflict. In the thrust and counterthrust of two impassioned opponents one senses the essence of what action is about: the movement of the human personality toward an adjustment with whatever tends to frustrate it. Complications, entangling influences, force the hero to fight harder and thus to prolong the period the adjustment must take. The lengthening of the conflict causes in the observer watching it the feeling of pleasurable worry called suspense, and it stretches mightily the whole sense of action. Action forced by a challenge, a will, and an effort to overcome—this is stuff with which dramatic games deal.

The general idea of dramatic action can be put into a nutshell by saying the action is a *series of connected changes experienced in the pursuit of a human adjustment.* Each change of feeling or thought causes a change of tension in the human organism. So the foregoing description of action has a corollary: *The complete action in a play is composed of a series of increasing and decreasing tensions leading to a climactic experience, a supreme change of tension.* At every moment the spectator senses a striving for new balance—by the hero or by some other character in the drama—he is sensing action, and he will continue to sense it until the final, crucial adjustment is achieved.

There are two general directions for dramatic action. One is outward, toward the environment. The other is inward, toward the individual. These directions of motion are affected by two others which express the urges to approach something, that is to attach oneself to another force; and to withdraw, that is detach oneself from the other force. The fundamental movements can be diagrammed this way.

Extension of the Individual		Attachment to an Object	
OUTWARD:	expanding	TOWARD:	approaching
	toward environment		*for attachment*
INWARD:	contracting	AWAY FROM:	withdrawing
	into oneself		*for detachment*

All are rooted in biology. Expanding and contracting are associated with the surging and ebbing of life. The characteristic expressions are seen especially in the movements of rising and sinking. The first green shoot from a plant seed pushes upward toward the sky. As long as sap rises from the roots to the top, the plant grows. When it dies, stricken by drought, too much rain, or disease, it shrivels and sinks downward to the earth again. The growing child lifts itself from a recumbent posture onto its hands and knees, then into an erect position on its feet. As the child becomes older it lifts its head and makes a final conquest of gravity by leaping, climbing, and dancing. When the man becomes feeble he sinks into himself, drops into a chair, lowers himself into bed, and finally goes down into a grave. In the same way, families, nations, and civilizations rise and fall.

Expanding and contracting may involve the enlargement and shrinking of an organism's whole feeling of existence, both physical and mental. Stretching out one's body and mind for new contacts in the world gives the organism a sense of growth. It means the pushing out of one's personal powers, also the reproducing of oneself in creative works. The shrinking organism inverts to itself, pulling away from outside contacts and denying its attention to any identity except its own.

Approaching and withdrawing are concerned with the movement of the human organism toward pleasurable things and away from hurtful ones. Man, like the beasts, is attracted toward good food, a comfortable shelter, and a desirable mate; and he is driven back by objects which threaten pain. In a more complex way man seeks to move toward wealth, beauty, honor, companionship, and self-respect and away from poverty, ugliness, degradation, loneliness, and shame. Nearly everything, physical or mental, which one does from rising in the morning till retiring at night is motivated by attractions and repulsions.

The fundamental movements described here do not create dramatic actions; they mark the directions of it. An examination of any group of successful plays clearly shows how the dramatic craftsman has used them to give shape to active effects.[1] In *Oedipus*, a man who has risen to a throne and the highest possible respect of a people sinks when he learns the truth about

1. See discussion on the playgoer as play-player and the performer as the playmaker and guide on p. 14.

himself. In *Macbeth*, the man rises and sinks. Most heroic tragedies, from the Greeks to the present, are built on the formula of up-to-down action. Romantic plays on the Cinderella theme reverse the action down-to-up. The difference of status here is symbolized by a difference of posture, from stooping over the ashes of a hearth to standing erect in a palace.

J. M. Barrie's *What Every Woman Knows* is a play of general expansion; so is Robert Sherwood's *Abe Lincoln in Illinois*. Henrik Ibsen's *An Enemy of the People*, Lillian Hellman's *The Children's Hour*, Eugene O'Neill's *The Hairy Ape*, and Paul Green's *The Field of God* are dramatizations of intensive contractions. In a way, *Oedipus*, a portrait of an exalted man sinking, is also the study of a man of expansive activity being driven back, back, into the narrow agony of an isolated mind. So is *King Lear*. If one wants an example from the present theatre, one can find it in Brecht's *The Good Woman of Setzuan* or Ionesco's *Rhinoceros*. Beckett's *Endgame* is a scene of contraction.

Romeo and Juliet is the story of two families that are trying to withdraw from each other and two young lovers who, reaching for each other, pull the rival groups together. Euripides' *Medea* and Sidney Howard's *The Silver Cord* are plays of separation, while Eugene O'Neill's *Anna Christie* and *Desire Under the Elms* are plays of coming together. Edward Albee's *Who's Afraid of Virginia Woolf?* is a drama of separation with some sense of union at the end. *The Glass Menagerie* reverses the directions. Many plays use combinations of movements, such as expansion *and* attachment, or expansion *and* detachment, and so on.

Much has been said in this chapter about the value of struggle. (Note the difference with regard to this requirement between the open-ended, no-plot episode and the conventional play, to which we are referring here. See Chapter I.) How really necessary is it in drama? The question has been debated at length by William Archer, John Howard Lawson, and others, and I have no desire to extend the argument. My own inclination is to stress the irreducible requirements of change and action—then to point out *how useful struggle is for bringing out these two factors.* How can one do without them? Struggle between two opposites provides the best means for effecting a swift, intense, and continuing interplay between a person and a segment of his environment. Therefore, it offers the most vigorous way for creating a sense of dramatic action. It also helps to reveal character. An individual engaged in conflict cannot sit still. He is bound to move. Movement makes him show the various facets of his nature. That is how the spectator is enabled to feel him and to live in him.

And of course if one is playing a game one is bound to be engaged in contest. This involves a form of struggle. (In *On Aggression,* one of the world's leading naturalists, Konrad Lorenz, affirms that aggression is a basic element of the natures of both animals and human creatures. The ape or the man who plays a game of life is bound to employ the action of struggling. It is a cultured factor of his everyday life and so must be a part of every playful imitation of it.) If one accepts the value of struggle one is compelled to recognize the importance of will. For some strange reason, this is a suspect word in certain areas of the theatre today. The Absurdist dramatists particularly like to proclaim the death of this attribute of man. Yet they find that in order to produce a sense of change and action in the spectator they have to use it. The Old Man and the Old Woman in Ionesco's *The Chairs* do not propose to do very much. But they do *will* to have an audience, they do *will* to have an orator, and they do *will* to leap into the sea. Neither of the two derelicts in Beckett's *Waiting for Godot* has a lofty ambition, but both *will* resolutely to wait. In the more genuinely active drama, the will is central and it is attached to proponent and opponent motions alike. Considerable will of this kind is exhibited in Ionesco's *The Lesson,* Pinter's *The Birthday Party,* and Genet's *The Balcony.*

There are, as we have already noted, many definitions of a play. For the spectators who are activists—and most spectators are— a drama is a triad: (a) a statement of a basic desire, (b) the visualization of an image of a fulfillment, and (c) *a willful effort to realize that image*. A continuity of willful effort makes action.

To repeat, one shift between differences of physical, mental, or emotional conditions makes *a change*. A sequence of such changes makes *action*. The more, and the quicker the changes in a certain scene the more active it usually seems to be. If one were to pick the most active parts of *Hamlet*, for instance, I think one would choose the early sequence on the ramparts, Hamlet's interviewing of his mother, his mousetrapping of the King, and the final dueling scene because in these parts the changes come forcefully and fast, one after another.

In the final analysis it is the grand changes, the master changes, which are the most important to dramatic effect. What the spectator coming to the theatre is looking for first of all is a *big experience* and this he gets only when he can participate, not in just little rises and falls, but in great ones extending over time and over physical and mental space. The little changes have their own values, but chiefly as they lead to a more extensive feeling of plunging toward catastrophe or of climbing toward exaltation. The climactic moment at the end of the journey, away down in defeat or away up in victory, is the one the spectator remembers most strongly afterwards; and this moment stands out for him when it is contrasted strongly with an opposite state before it.

If in prospect or retrospect the experience of a striking change seems to be logically connected with the whole situation one is observing, one recognizes it as being arresting, dramatic. If it cannot be so connected, it is shocking, or at best, absurd. One can imagine the kind of effect which would be produced if Nora's game with the children in A *Doll's House* should be interrupted, not by Krogstad but by a London policeman. Krogstad belongs, because he is an associate of Nora's family. Hamlet is kin to the Ghost who surprises him. What he talks about is connected with their joint affairs. Laertes' quick anger and Ophelia's startling madness are related to the course of the other tragic events at Elsinore. Because they are connected they are dramatic.

In any designed composition, then, dramatic effects must be

built on concepts of appropriateness. Oedipus' fall from his eminence is a progressive one; there are many smaller changes working toward the great one. Every one of them, however, is connected somehow with Oedipus' kingship over Thebes. The Emperor Jones in Eugene O'Neill's play is a different kind of ruler, but his sovereignty over a West Indian island provides a comparable line of unity for his story. At the beginning he is a monarch indeed, stately, arrogant, and assured; at the end he has reverted to primitive savagery, quivering with fear, and is killed as the result of his own superstitions. What gives depth to the sense of tragedy in his case is the image it carries of the emperor who once was.

Maggie in J. M. Barrie's *What Every Woman Knows* passes through many reversals, but they are all connected with her growth as a wife. At the opening of her drama she is an eager, but (apparently) quite undesirable woman; at the close, a valuable and beloved companion. Between the poles of her development is a central thread of evolution which binds the contrasting points together. *An Enemy of the People* has moments of success and failure, all related to Dr. Stockman's sense of duty to his community. The doctor is free, but restless with the feeling that he has not yet given complete expression to his urge for service; then he is closed in, but calmed with the satisfaction that his conscience has had its fulfillment. Lincoln in *Abe Lincoln in Illinois* possesses a sense of Destiny, an awareness of a kind of call from his country. He is a raw country boy; then a growing statesman with the glow of greatness beginning to shine in him. Both Stockman and Lincoln move a long way in their lives, but whatever they do and whatever they say belong to unity. They each take part in a progress from one opposite to the other.

The changes in the theatre which cause dramatic effects take an infinite variety of forms. Many of them however, tend to fall into typical patterns of which the four most common are:

(a) *A quick rise of stimulation.* One hears a clap of thunder, or sees a bolt of lightning. One suddenly becomes aware of a face at the window. One feels an unexpected hand on one's shoulder. The first impact causes the dramatic feeling. If the thunder, the lightning, or the fall of the hand is repeated, it soon ceases to be dramatic. An example of an effective rise in stimulation in a play is that caused, as we have seen, in *The Little Foxes* when Horace, after listening quietly to Regina's declaration of her hatred for him, suddenly reaches his trembling hand toward the bottle of heart medicine, upsets it, and hoarsely begs her to get the other bottle.

(b) A *quick cessation of stimulation*. Silence in a house after a door has been closed may be quite arresting. A dancer in a ballet suddenly stopping his movement may attract as much attention as one leaping into action. In a similar way, Regina's stillness after her pressure on Horace can be impressive. When Horace excitedly upsets the bottle of medicine and cries for help, the spectator expects her also to do something active. Instead, she stands motionless and silent.

(c) A *quick alteration in the level of stimulation*. A marked increase of speed in an automobile or a decrease of noise in an auditorium, or a sharp change from height toward depth, or from heat toward cold, or from brilliance toward darkness, can be dramatic. In a like manner, the accelerating fury of Hamlet's rapier thrusts at Laertes, after he suspects he is being plotted against, is arresting.

(d) A *quick shift in the kind of stimulation*. Through a device of lighting, perhaps, a pink costume turns blue; the blinking of an electric light fades into the sound of a bell; a taste changes to an odor. These impressions also can be striking. An example in another form is the quick shift of the pioneers in a play about the early frontier from a scene of feasting to a rush for their guns on the call of "Indians."

Analogous to the effects caused by physical changes are the effects which spring from (a) a quick upsurge of thought, (b) a quick failure of thought, (c) a quick shift in the intensity of thought, and (d) a quick alteration in the kind of thought. Seated relaxed in an easy chair, one suddenly remembers an engagement; under pressure of a critical test, one forgets an important fact; spurred by the threat in a tight problem, one accelerates one's thinking on it; struck by the new meaning of a phrase uttered, one turns from an expression of disbelief to a conviction. In each case it is the *feeling state* caused that is important. The feeling marks the personal readjustment of the person experiencing the change. Unless a feeling of some kind results from the change, there is no effect. The feeling must be clear; the sharper and stronger the feeling, the more definite is the effect.

Experiments in the psychological laboratory have shown that a disturbing stimulus, like a small electric shock or the sound of a buzzer, increases muscular tension; and that this new tension is greatest when it is accompanied by anticipation. That is, waiting for the shock or the buzzing causes the person expecting it to get all keyed up about it, then to respond more violently when it comes. Anyone who has waited for the burst of a gun or the explosive ring of a telephone bell can verify this tendency to tense in suspense, then to tense still more in the actual change.

The dramatic artist finds here a clear answer to the old question as to whether in a dramatic design a surprise effect is more potent than an anticipated one. Generally speaking more force seems to be attached to a change leaning on suspense. A classic example of the power of anticipation is the scene in *The School for Scandal* in which the audience waits with excitement for the moment when Sir Peter Teazle will discover his wife hiding behind the screen. Several times Teazle starts to peek. Each time he is prevented the spectator becomes more excited about a final revelation.

From the point of view of a broad definition of theatrical effect could a performance of such a conversational play as *Waiting for Godot* be regarded as active? The answer is "Of course (comparatively speaking)—as long as the dialogue is affected by a vigorous bounce." If a play contains a lot of changes (of any kind) and these changes are made to occur in a lively, continuing sequence, it will be active. *Godot* is helped by the bits of unexpected business with Estragon's shoes and by the striking movements attending the entrance of Pozzo and Lucky. At best, however, this could never be regarded as being more than a *relatively* active play. It is limited, as we have already noted, by an absence of plot, and by the very small amount of physical stirring-about. For this reason, we tend to think of *Godot* as being, all in all, like the rest of Beckett's plays, rather static. That is what the author wanted it to be. Static, but not so static as to prevent the spectator from listening to the dialogue.

Plays of adventure usually require considerable bodily movement. The more intellectual dramas demand less; but even those that lean markedly toward a quiet interchange of words need at least some physical mobility, because visible movement alerts the attention of the audience as well as helps the actor to convey his thoughts. *The Member of the Wedding* is a "quiet" play. It would seem even quieter if it were just heard on the radio.

The playwright gets at the heart of action by working on an inward thinking and feeling of the characters in his drama. So long as he can keep these turning one way, then another, his play will be bound to seem to have action. A nervous sequence of reversals cultivated just for their own sake, however, can be active in a spurious sort of way, yet be quite uninteresting. It can be annoying for the spectator if the elements seem to be simply jumping up and down or spinning around without going in any direction. The surest way the playwright has for making the units of his action appear to progress toward a culminating point is to have clearly in mind at all times just what is the central issue, and to see that throughout the action the dominant figure of his story (the protagonist) is moved by a strong drive toward the fulfillment of his want.

The performing artist's grasp of physical design reaches beyond the elements of his bodily and speech patterns seen in isolation, to the part they must play in the total stage composition. He observes the pantomime of the other actors in the set and takes care not to ape it in shape or rhythm. He listens to his companions' speech and makes his own pitch and inflectional forms have an individuality which will keep them separate from the others'. With the help of the costumer, he sees that the color of his clothes does not "melt into" the color of the scenic background, that his make-up does not fade from view when he stands in front of a window or a set of draperies. With the guiding assistance of the director, he strives to get variety of position and posture with respect to the people among whom he sits, stands, and walks. He does all this, not because he wishes to call undue attention to himself, but because he knows that the stage scene has life for the playgoer only when each member of the dramatic ensemble maintains a distinct personality and keeps alive the play of interchange between character and character. This is the way the game of theatre is played. The spectator feels himself into every part of the action, so he feels as if he had, as it were, a prowess of his own in creating dramatic adventure.

IV. A Sense of Excitement

—FEELING

The sense of aliveness experienced by the spectator springs from an awareness of change—change continuing, in progress toward more change—thus making action. Change is the first and crucial factor in the spectator's response to a dramatic performance. But the sense of aliveness, the sense of change, of action, will have very little influence on the person engaged in a game of theatre unless it is suffused with a feeling. Without feeling, accelerated living, however it may be inflected, still remains not much more than a kind of sharp but essentially nervous twitter. It is the feeling that makes changeful action glow with meaningfulness.

What about the place of rational thought in all this, someone may ask. That is important, but it does not come first. The primary fact of man's nature is feeling. That was true in the days of his earliest savagery; it is equally true today. Emotion is the innermost, and so the truly dramatic part of every human creature. "Emotions accompany all our instinctive acts," says the biologist James G. Needham, "and it is emotions that move us; not reason. Reason is too cold, too slow, too uncertain in its conclusions and its operations. Reason uses all, knows all, but does not rule. Reason sits in the outlook tower, but the seat of control is elsewhere."[1] Says Alfred North Whitehead: "In the study of ideas, it is necessary to remember, that insistence on hard-headed clarity issues from sentimental feeling, as it were a mist, cloaking the perplexities of fact. . . . Our reasonings grasp at straws for premises and float on gossamers for deductions."[2] The function of logic is to help people make their wishes orderly and to assist in the fulfillment of them; the driving force everywhere—even in the act of exercising logic itself—is feeling.

Grown people are sometimes afraid to acknowledge their feel-

1. James G. Needham, *About Ourselves* (Lancaster, Penn.: The Jacques Cattell Press, 1941), p. 223.
2. Alfred North Whitehead, *Adventures of Ideas* (New York: The Macmillan Company, 1933), p. 91.

ings; children are not. They like them and enjoy showing them. Mrs. Francis Clark Sayers, long superintendent of work with children in the New York Public Library, has noted that children love to conjure up things that make them feel; they even like things that frighten them. As a librarian, she recalls how children approached her saying, "Give me a book that will scare me to death." Grown persons are similar to children in desiring to escape from the common world of reason and to experience emotions, *provided that they can have the emotions under conditions of control.* The place where they can enjoy them most freely (without any fear of their extending themselves into complications beyond a specified time and place) is the theatre. The experiencing of lively feelings is fun when it occurs in the spirit of controllable play!

Human feelings operate in the theatre on three levels. On the highest are the emotions. Below them are other feelings which are not so insistent but which have importance because they lead up to and give support to the emotions. The first are sensations, the second the general feelings of pleasure and unpleasure. Sensations are created when physical stimuli stir the sensory nerves. One sees, hears, smells, tastes, or touches. One is aware of the sunshine or of a fall of the temperature. Hamlet is experiencing a sensation when he observes on the rampart of the castle of Elsinore: "The air bites shrewdly; it is very cold."

Sensations are of course the most common things in the world. Everybody has them all day long, he cannot avoid them. Most sensations, however, are quite mild, like the impression made by the weight of a coat on one's back, by the pressure of the floor against one's feet, or by the sight of the same old path leading up to the same old front door. They are taken so much for granted that if one were asked to give a description of them, he would have difficulty supplying it. A person utters a remark about a sensation only when it is strong enough to force itself into his conscious mind. This tends to occur when there is a shift in the sensation, that is, when it rises, sinks away, alters its intensity, or changes its form.

In the theatre, stimuli are provided that make *noticeable* sensations. Spectators come to the playhouse for a *sensory feast*; tradition has made the theatre a house of spectacle. It is significant that sensuously the most lavish theatre is found now in those countries where abstract science, philosophy, and religion have tended through the years to diminish the value of the human body. The senses of people in those places are so often starved that they must return to the playhouses to get them fed. To meet the playgoer's hunger for visual and auditory stimulation the artist heightens the pale color of the actors' faces making the women more beautiful, the men more virile. He dresses their bodies in bright fabrics with strongly tactile textures. He paints brilliant settings for the actors' background, trains them to walk rhythmically and to speak in well-modulated tones, and accompanies their actions with musical instruments. All of this is done, first of all, for the purpose of satisfying sensory desires.

A general feeling of pleasure or displeasure is more resonant than the sensation; it makes more of the organism vibrate. It commonly stirs up the whole body. One has a feeling of displeasure when one is hungry, thirsty, lonesome, restless, sad; one has a feeling of pleasure because one is well-fed, peaceful, or happy. The hungriness, restlessness, or peacefulness themselves are feelings. They are "good" or "bad" in reference to the absence or presence of pain in them. The pleasant and unpleasant states of feeling in a person involve a change not only in his sensory but also in his inner organs; his stomach, his heart, and his breathing apparatus. They are normally associated with changes of bodily posture. A person with a feeling of displeasure or pleasure in a play will say something comparable to what Juliet's old nurse utters when she is tired: "I am a-weary . . . how my bones ache!" or what a poetic young girl remarks when she is buoyant: "I step on mountains, touch the stars." While an individual says the first she will tend to droop; while the latter will lift herself up as if she were actually on a mountain reaching skyward.

The general feelings of pleasure and displeasure grow out of sensation, of course, and they reflect the attitude of the person toward his sensory experience. He is aware of heat on his thumb, pulls it back, and sees he has touched the stove; he has an unpleasant feeling of pain. An odor of spoiled food assails his nose. The nerves twitch and the nostrils contract; he has a feeling of discomfort. His tongue is immersed in a flavorsome liquid. The beverage is "delicious"; the man's whole body vibrates with pleasure. In the person having them, all of these feelings are connected with the sense of lowered or heightened vitality.

An emotion is similar to a general feeling except that it is more focused, more intense, and more active. What causes an unpleasant or pleasant feeling causes also an emotional feeling when the blocking or releasing of a human urge is increased in force and speed. Apprehension becomes fear, annoyance becomes anger, fondness becomes love, gladness becomes joy. It is the man filled with passion who exclaims: "A plague o' both your houses!" or "Free! I'm free!" The tendency toward posturing becomes now an inclination to act. When one is hit by an assailant, one experiences a flash of rage and has an impulse to hit back. When one is confronted suddenly with a menacing object, one has a stab of fear and wants to cry out about it. If Mercutio were able to move when he says "A plague o' both your houses!" he would draw his sword and drive from him those who have hurt him. The young man who shouts his freedom may feel a desire to express his joy by leaping into the air.

But the inclination to movement need not actually express itself openly. This tends to be true in the case of the kind of emotional experience that springs from a quick shift in mental attitudes. If the philosophical tenet one has long held with affection is suddenly vindicated—or suddenly violated—one will have an emotion about it. If a rule of moral conduct one cherishes is praised or is sneered at by another, one will have an emotion. So, often, a research physicist, assiduously tracking down some point of fact in nuclear reaction, finds his path gloriously opened up for him or frustratingly closed. While these changes in a man's thinking experience are obviously mental, they are not only mental. What in them causes emotion is usually a whole group of factors having to do with the man's way of living. The security or the loss of a certain kind of belief may affect in prospect the entire course of one's future actions. Someone else's attitude toward one's rules of conduct can alter materially one's later association with society. The discovery or the loss of one bit of information by a scholar can mean the difference between the respectful or contemptuous response of his colleagues, or involve a promotion—and through that promotion the purchase of a car or the money for a summer in Canada. However it is viewed, the mental change becomes emotional just as soon as it raises in the human organism the need for a new, swift adjustment. And this adjustment almost always implies some kind of action sensed, if not in overt movement, at least in imagination.

An expression of a general feeling or of an emotion provides a sign of the way the human organism is living: it shows what success it is having in its efforts to exercise its powers, secure or expand them. When a restriction is imposed on its powers it has an entirely different feeling from the one it has when a restriction is lifted. The only time the organism has no feeling at all is when it is living perfectly efficiently and is aware of neither a restriction nor a release—or when it is dead!

An individual may experience general satisfaction or general disappointment and do nothing very specifically as a result of it. On the other hand, a person who experiences fear, anger, or love is almost certain to show his feeling in movement forcefully. For each emotion there is naturally an active image: weeping, laughing, jumping, shouting, striking, embracing, trembling, blushing. These are signs of human living experiences in their most vigorous states.

All this might take place in the everyday world, or in a play in the theatre. For illustration, there are two scenes in Tennessee Williams' *A Streetcar Named Desire* which show clearly how quick release of a block to desire, and a sudden imposition of a block to desire, cause emotion expressed in action. The scenes involve Blanche DuBois and Mitch, the big, shy, but good-hearted friend of the Kowalskis. In the first scene, Blanche, defeated and depressed, and desperately lonely, has gone out with Mitch wishing, but not very hopefully, that maybe she can work up some kind of friendship with this equally lonesome man. The evening has been miserable. On this hot night Blanche has been unable to be the gay woman she has wanted to be. Neither of the two has been able to talk much. Blanche believes that Mitch has been terribly disappointed in her. They have finally arrived at her apartment, both with the sense that their effort at companionship has been a failure.

Then, unaccountably, Mitch has begun to talk—clumsily, almost inarticulately at first, but enough to make Blanche perceive that, after all, he does like her. He speaks to her in a way he has never spoken before. She has a sudden rush of joy. With a soft cry she huddles in his arms. She draws and releases her breath in long, grateful sobs. "Sometimes," she says, "there's God—so quickly!"

For a few weeks Blanche is very happy. Then there comes an end to the feeling of release. Her brother-in-law Stanley has told Mitch some of the more sordid details of her past and the big man suddenly returns to the apartment hurt and confused. Blanche tries valiantly to straighten out their relationship; she exerts herself one last time. Then she gives up in a rage. She tells Mitch to leave. He stands staring at her. Blanche rushes to the window and cries wildly, "Fire! Fire!"

These two short scenes (supported by what precedes them) contain all the factors of sensation, physically and mentally induced feelings of pleasure and displeasure, and finally emotion, that we have described. Blanche's culminating state of hysteria is caused by the sudden return of her vision of the meaningless future she has striven so hard to escape.

The playgoer, living in imagination Blanche's role in these two scenes, will feel the feelings depicted in the play. He will share Mitch's feelings in the same way. One very important thing to note about feelings is the relation that exists between the parts. All feeling sequences start, as we have said, with a sensation. Lo-

renzo and Jessica in *The Merchant of Venice* are walking in the
grounds of Portia's Belmont when Lorenzo remarks sensuously,

> How sweet the moonlight sleeps upon this bank.
> Here will we sit and let the sound of music creep in our ears.

The two young people look and listen, and what they apprehend
about the night and the sounds from the musicians' instruments
creates a mood in them. They make love to each other.

Sensation in everyday man or the playgoer can be the end of a
feeling experience. It may go on into a general feeling; or it may
go still further into an emotion. A homely example from outside
the theatre will help to illustrate this progression. Let us think
of a young boy on his way to a picnic. He is walking along a
country path. He senses the stretch of his muscles, the softness
of the turf under his feet, and the coolness of the breeze across
his face. He takes pleasure in his walking. Now he turns his
ankle. Pleasure turns to displeasure. If the sprain is slight, the
feeling will be mild. He may continue his journey without suffering anything more violent than a little annoyance at his awk-
wardness. If, however, the turn has caused a sharp pain, it will
probably make the boy angry and he will cry aloud. The emotion will be intensified if the boy discovers that the foot is
really badly wrenched and realizes that the remainder of what
had promised to be a fine afternoon is now ruined. Perhaps he
will be unable to get to the picnic at all. He will be denied the
pleasurable experience of eating a good lunch, of seeing his
friends, and of participating in the baseball game planned as the
crowning event of the afternoon. The thought of all this frustration makes him furious! He slams the ground with his fists!

The boy in this incident has had a mental frustration built
on top of a physical frustration; his emotional experience consequently is twofold. Now let us imagine a further complication.
He has dragged himself out to a public road, and is seated on a
stump, nursing his ankle with his hands, and muttering angrily
to himself. He hears a car approach. He lifts his eyes. The boy

can scarcely believe what he sees: the car is filled with several of his friends, and heaped up in clear view on the rear seat are the picnic provisions and the sports equipment! This promised deliverance is so unexpected that the boy has a burst of joy. He leaps to his feet in spite of his injured ankle and starts yelling excitedly! But the persons in the car do not recognize him among the bushes, perhaps, so they speed on. Now the individual by the roadside has been triply frustrated. At this moment he feels his pain with even greater keenness than he did before because he has had a glimpse of happy release from it, which is now lost. He will most certainly express himself in some way both pantomimically and vocally. Since there is no one around to look at him disapprovingly, the boy will probably stamp the ground with his good foot and sob unrestrainedly.

Only when the experience of frustration or facilitation becomes strong enough, let me emphasize, does it go over into the realm of emotions. This is an important point for the playmaker-performer to understand, because inexperienced craftsmen in the theatre often fail to see the difference between two steps of feeling. Theatre deals fundamentally with *emotions*, but many dramatic artists never arrive at these at all. (A striking failure in so many of the works of our time, many playwrights of today tend to be afraid of emotion. Avant-gardists, dedicated increasingly to objective approaches, frankly express a distaste for it. It is my conviction that when they speak this way they are ignoring the deeper wishes of their audiences.) The greatest difference between general feelings and emotions, let us say again, lies in their motile qualities. It is true that a person feeling an emotion may refrain from a giving a visible expression to it, but the impulse to movement is always there. It is illuminating to note that actual murders and suicides do not usually spring from general feelings but from emotions. There may have been a long sequence of sensations and general feelings building up to the event but the final act is set off by some kind of emotional shock.

In every play of strong feeling the element of time presses heavily on the protagonist. There are deadlines to be met. Decisions cannot be put off. The temporal push creates a condition of urgency, and the more the time margin is reduced—compressed—as the drama progresses, the more painful becomes the sense of the holding force. So now it takes only a little extra squeeze to make a feeling of unbearable restriction, and only a little relaxing to get the sense of a big liberation. The protagonist jumps emotionally into action with each change of tension. (All through this discussion we are describing the progress of the playgoer's feelings, of course, right along with the stage character's feelings he is observing.)

Variable tension, then, is the core of sentient experience in the theatre. The experience begins with sensation and it develops with frustrations and liberations. The result on one level is a general feeling of pleasantness or unpleasantness; on another it is an emotion. The more violent and the more sudden the application or removal of an inhibiting force at the end of preparatory action and the greater the climate of urgency in which this operates, the sharper is the passion generated. (This condition of the character is not only apprehended by the playgoer objectively; it is also lived through by him subjectively, as well.)

Thus on the level of craftsmanship we come to the problem of theatrical design. The artist in the playhouse, determined to affect the spectators as broadly as possible, starts his composition (whatever its form—a playscript, a costume, a stage setting or a piece of acting) with sensation. He makes an appeal for attention by presenting the spectator with some stimulus *different from what he has been experiencing*. That is why the theatre auditorium, in contrast with the bustling streets outside, is quiet. That is why the lights are lowered and soft music is played. After the artist has caught the interest of the man in the auditorium he holds it with many other sensory appeals. He fills the stage with fine, bold lines, bright colors, strong textures, striking sounds that excite the observer's perceptions. If the artist is dealing with human bodies and voices, he provides movements of attack and response which create images of human energy in action.

Through the sensation, the artist arrives at the general feelings. To develop them he arranges tensions and releases made by forceful frustrations or facilitations of strong drives. He makes the painful ones by blocking the drives and the pleasant ones by removing blocks.

But the artist knows that gentle, slowly growing feelings are not intrinsically active, and therefore not fully dramatic. So the artist tries to find ways for intensifying the general feelings into emotions. He discovers that he can do this by working for quick, strong changes in the relation between the persons and objects on the stage, and through them in the feeling of the spectator in the auditorium. He finds that the surest way to create an emotion is to let an urge flow freely, then suddenly to block it, or to dam up an urge until it accumulates force, then suddenly release it. The most effective way to do this, he learns, is to bring two dramatic personalities together in conflict. In physics, when one solid mass collides with another, a form of energy is generated which we call heat. In the same way, when one human personality pushes another, a form of energy is generated which we call drama. Drama can be defined then as the emotional feeling of tension (frustration) or release (freedom) expressed in action.

From beginning to end, what the artist deals with is the stuff of human life in the process of change. "If living is anything," remarks an eminent psychologist, "it is dramatic: the most significant and interesting things about life are those episodes in which the demand is for some novel mode of activity, some readjustment of one's behavior to meet the requirements of new or unusual situations. As he grows from puling infancy to manhood's estate, the human being is faced day by day with new conditions, changes of material surrondings, new groups of human faces; and it is a truism that his mental development is shown in how he meets these ever-changing circumstances by remolding and reshaping his own reactions to them."[3]

Here are the elements out of which the artist builds his play-making composition. They are the stuff which, when prodded by

3. John Frederick Dashiell, *Fundamentals of General Psychology* (Boston: Houghton Mifflin Company, 1937), p. 28.

swift change and vigorous action, create that sense of excitement that the playgoer comes to the playhouse to experience. They make him think, they make him move—implicitly. They make him cry and laugh—actually. Thus together they exercise him all over.

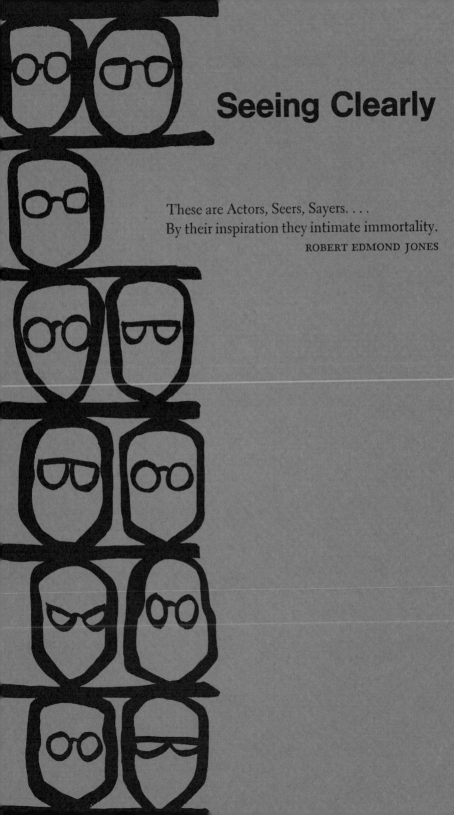

Seeing Clearly

These are Actors, Seers, Sayers. . . .
By their inspiration they intimate immortality.

ROBERT EDMOND JONES

V. A *Sense of Illumination*
—ASPECTS

While clearly there is a first and most compelling wish that brings the playgoer to the playhouse, a desire for excitement, surely there is a second, lesser but still vigorous wish, the desire for illumination. The satisfaction of this second wish involves both intellectual and emotional approaches. A complete treatment of these would take space beyond the appropriate limits of this book. I shall try in the following few pages of this and the following chapter to indicate just a few of the more important of the approaches.

Let us remind ourselves that the kind of play we are discussing here is not the one prepared for reading quietly beside the fire in one's home but the kind devised to stir up a lively visual and auditory response in a theatre, one that produces an immediate effect on all the faculties of the playgoer's muscular and glandular system—only in part on his mind. The emphasis is kinetic rather than deliberate. The playmaker constructing a play for such an instant fully-living reaction cannot start from scratch to build an intellectual framework for his composition, from the bottom up; he has to count on certain emotionally-affected premises held by the playgoer, and to go from there. This is like setting up the bricks on a foundation already laid.

This does not mean for a moment that a playgoer cannot appreciate original thinking in the playhouse. It means only that the producing artist has to put his ideas deftly *on top of certain deeply felt, not always readily expressible, convictions already embraced by the playgoer's inner personality*—that and a wish to have those convictions verified or cultivated by challenge.

In the intellectual field then, the dialogue between the craftsman and the spectator is not much affected by abstract argument. It is carried on by a series of confrontations of sentient attitudes, attitudes picturized in human images seen and heard. These are what we shall try roughly to identify.

We shall start with a broad look at the playgoer's commonly *inherent* attitudes.

One of the chief distinguishing marks of the human creature is his insatiable curiosity about himself and his fellows. Long ago the American humorist, Clarence Day, author of *Life with Father*, wrote a book, *This Simian World*, in which he asked the question, why was it that the descendants of the most unlikely family of beasts, the monkeys, propelled themselves into the domination of the earth? His conclusion, arrived at with admitted reluctance, was that the cause was the monkeys' propensity for sticking their noses into everything—the growth of bananas, the change of the wind, the behavior of each other's wives, the scandalous character of the baboons in the other part of the forest—then chattering to each other about it!

It is only people today, not animals, who concern themselves about the exercise and the response to art, and the reason for this doubtless exists in the fact that art provides the most effective device there is for communicating the nature of man to man. It satisfies curiosity, a supra-simian curiosity, perhaps. Natures reveal themselves in music, painting, and architecture. They tend to be strongest in the descriptive and imitative arts, such as the novel and the theatre; most especially the theatre, since it shows human character not only implicitly in verbal delineations, but explicitly in sensible forms and sounds. There are very many questions that the playgoer asks in the playhouse. The most important are these three: "What kind of being am I?" "What kind of beings are they?" "How do individuals achieve through games the things they want from each other?" Among the many points of search, these are pre-eminent.

One of the principal attractions of going to see a play is, then, the opportunity it affords the observer to project himself playfully into the lives of other sentient people and to find there the ways in which they in their personal transactions with each other reveal things about themselves they had not intended to show. A knowledge of the hidden motives of human behavior is interesting to everybody, yet these motives are not readily accessible in our daylight world. In the playhouse people are presented with such special challenges that they are forced to open up and thus reveal themselves. We recognize the need for the wearing of masks outside the theatre; life would be intolerable if we went around showing our naked faces regularly. But the mutual observance of the courtesy of reticence is not required in the house where we play games freely. Here we can demand that the masks be removed so that we can easily see, and so better understand how basic reactions between people operate.

In his novel *Look Homeward Angel*, Thomas Wolfe describes the loneliness which is the common pain of man, and suggests how this loneliness impels him ceaselessly to touch, and to try to obtain responses from, the people around him, all of whom suffer the same kind of loneliness as he:

Naked and alone we came into exile. In her dark womb we did not know our mother's face; from the prison of her flesh have we come into the unspeakable and incommunicable prison of this earth.

Which of us has known his brother? Which of us has looked into his father's heart? Which of us has not remained forever prison-pent? Which of us is not forever a stranger and alone?[1]

The playhouse provides a means for the reaching of contacts. In the playhouse they are vicarious contacts it is true, but in their way they give the comfort of actual contacts, and they give us hints on the recognition and the use of the contacts of the real world.

The concern about human contact starts young. Parents observe that when an infant begins to grow up, a part of his normal stimulus-hunger turns into a recognition-hunger. He wants to have his presence—his physical and psychic powers, his potential contributions to, and demands of, the community—noted by other humans. He soon learns that the most effective way

1. Thomas Wolfe, *Look Homeward, Angel* (New York: Charles Scribner's Sons, 1929), p. 2.

to draw attention to himself is to give attention to others. So he develops a game of giving and receiving what Dr. Eric Berne call "strokes." He is ready to play at this anytime it would seem to be advantageous. The baby coos, he smiles, he pats his mother's face. A stroke is an act implying the recognition of another human presence. Two people meet and through certain signals communicate to each other: "I'll stroke you if you'll stroke me." Dr. Berne says, "An exchange of strokes is the unit of social intercourse." This intercourse is necessary for the well-being of an individual's bodily and mental equilibrium. It is summarized in the colloquialism, "If you are not stroked, your spinal chord will shrivel up."

In the playful surroundings of the playhouse a spectator has an opportunity to observe the edifying actions of selected figures exchanging strokes in the pursuit of social aims. Better still, the spectator imagines himself sensuously into their bodies and minds and thus experiences directly the tensions and releases occasioned by the moves and countermoves of the stage characters' gamesmanship. The sensations for the spectator are both instructive and entertaining.

The playhouse provides a place where a playgoer can renew his insight into causes and effects. He feels the values of relationships. He participates in the asking and answering of questions about desire and satisfaction in different conditions. What he gets out of these experiences may not be really very new at all—perhaps the playgoer long ago found the answers to questions now being asked, but time and the unforeseen complications of his own life have blurred them and he wishes now to see the answers again, redefined. Some of them he will wish to see in this way over and over again.

What the spectator wants in the end is not so much the *facts* of knowledge as the *sense* of knowledge—what he can make a part, as it were, of his own bones, muscles, and blood stream. If he wished to obtain just facts, he would go to a library. The playhouse, unlike the other source, is emotionally oriented; so what he gets here is something more than the shape of facts. It is a feeling of being *on top of facts*—of being so clearsighted after attending the theatre that he can walk among his fellows now without confusion, keenly perceptive of why he and they are the way they are, and why he and they do what they do. In every way now he is superior to what he sees.

A primary function of the dramatic artist then is to put representative human facts (and speculations) into sensible images. No playwright was more aware of this truth than Bernard Shaw. He was impelled to satisfy his desire to write out his philosophical convictions by composing essays which he called Prefaces, but he knew clearly that his arguments on socialism, the power of money, religion, and the training of children would be widely persuasive only in living characters on a stage. So he wrote his ideas into plays. Perhaps the artist will regard his creation as a "revelation," and perhaps the man in the audience will accept it as such. Actually, of course, let us repeat, what the man in the audience gets mostly is a clarification of thoughts which are intrinsically his own. The dramatist, assuming a Jovian attitude, looks through a mass of disorderly details, picks out from a single perspective what appears to him to be the salient, most interesting, most provocative points, and makes them vivid and emphatic. He settles conflicts. He resolves inconsistencies. He proportions elements and ties them together in such a way as to make them present a unified, living idea. Then he sweeps away out of sight all the clutter which he feels would be distracting.

The playmaker presents on the stage the image of an old man, once a successful businessman, a salesman. Then, the salesman polished his shoes brightly and put on a smile. His associates liked him. He worked hard. He had a good family. He loved his wife and was proud of his two sons. Now, the man is disintegrating. For the spectator the playmaker asks the question, why has this individual, at one time so much on top of the world, sunk so low? The playmaker dees not answer directly, but by word and action—implicitly by sensuous means—he suggests the reply. The salesman has concerned himself so much with the outward appearance of things, especially the outward appearance of himself—the smile, the shoeshine, the hearty manner in the hotel bedroom, ignoring the fundamentally creative elements in himself and his friends—that the aging of the outward shell has left him nothing genuine to fall back on inside of himself. Thus, the playgoer, feeling himself into the progress of the old salesman's experiences, senses himself into the answer to the question originally asked.

When a playwright has an observation he wants to express—or when he wishes to plead a cause he personally has a feeling about—he embodies his point of view in one or more of the characters of his script and makes him or them act out the belief in such a way as to draw the spectator into it. If by this means the playwright seduces the mind of the spectator powerfully enough, he *may* change that mind not just temporarily but permanently; at least a little.

But this he can do only with the conscious or unconscious consent of the spectator. The playwright who wants to "sell" the idea of living life with extraordinary intensity may have to start with the common premise that "if you burn your candle at both ends it won't last long," as if it were the most reasonable assumption in the world that a long life is always desirable—then develop gradually a complementary thought that the length of a life is not as important as the brilliance of the flame you generate while you live that life, even if you shorten it. So the playwright composes the images of a Romeo and Juliet story. The two young people would like passionately to live out forever their wondrous love for each other. But the artist, as the wise onlooker, suggests that their present attachment is too perfect to have in it any really lasting power in this imperfect world. So he makes the two young people die before they suffer disillusionment. Are they not fortunate? he asks. The spectator replies, yes!

The artist helps the onlooker to see in a new way how certain personalities endowed with strong feelings in a given set of circumstances will seek by means of "strokes" to balance out the forces which disturb them, and how this effort at resolving their problem inevitably causes conflict. First, the situation indicates the promise of a fight—then there is the fight. After that there is a third step, a resolution. On the stage, this last phase of human relationship is likely to be the most fascinating of all because in real life the final adjustment of a conflict tends to be so drawn out, and to become so mixed up with cross conflicts, that one cannot see any pattern in it. The nondramatic Hamlet is often unable to work out his dilemma at all. Thus he must live out his miserable existence in a chronic state of dull resentment. On the stage, Hamlet gets his problem finally resolved. He dies, it is true, but he dies with his mind blessedly free—his own. The ending is not a "happy" one, but it is intellectually patterned. Dark confusions have been removed. It is good!

Traditional drama—that is, drama long cherished by the majority of playgoers—has looked for the truth of man in the unique part of him. To express this element of humanity in its most vivid colors the traditional artist picks characters that are like other men with respect to the existence of a personal uniqueness, but are "*more than that.*" When the dramatic artist deals with such people, he feels that he is dealing most distinctly with human truths. If he is successful, the spectator feels exhilarated. He is seeing into something wonderfully alive. Says Robert Sherwood: "The Theatre is the spiritual home of one who . . . requires and demands expression of great faith." Shakespeare, and long before him Sophocles, wrote about the "wonders of man." Brooks Atkinson speaks of "peeks at immortality."

Modern apostles of the painful absurdity of life like to take a different approach. They find that the primarily true facts of a human being are his loneliness and his inarticulateness. Says Tennessee Williams: "It is not the essential dignity but the ambiguity of man that I think needs to be considered." Eugene Ionesco feels that "social man is hell; other people are hell; if only one could do without them!" Which attitude will the playgoer favor? The choice is his. No one can force him to take one or the other.

Conditions right now are not of the kind to evoke grand

themes in the theatre. In the golden days, playmakers and play-goers together liked to celebrate the freedom of the human will. This was a favorite topic of the ancient Greeks, the Elizabethans, and the Frenchmen of the time of Racine. Things have changed since then. Darwin has shown that man is an animal, so he cannot look to find much divinity in his nature. Freud has convinced us that the decisions in a man's life are conditioned by an unconscious over which he has little control. That has made us even less sure of the quality of the will. The concept of the tragic sense as an ennobling force depends on a trust in the free movement of that will. Two big recent wars and the machine-dominated mass society to which they helped give birth have tended further to diminish the figures of free men in command of their actions.

This is what historians and critics are telling us today. Maybe it is fortunate that they are not always believed. The core of the human mind is tough. Having lost something of his faith in the benevolent orderliness of the universe on which he once leaned for his guidance, a resolute individual still keeps his respect and his love of the universe's energy and strives to partake of it. And from his belief in this energy he derives a sort of wistful but stubborn conviction about his own power to affect his fate. This is the existentialist's attitude. Jean-Paul Sartre has phrased the thought: "Man is condemned to be free."

But if, by and large, we have had to give up our trust in the magnitudinous aspects of classic tragedy, we still have comedy; at least of a sort. Walter Kerr in *Tragedy and Comedy* contends that grand comedy is the other side, the shadow as it were, of grand tragedy. There can be truly vigorous comedy only when there is vigorous tragedy. Nevertheless, we do have a lot of little comedies today. Comedy is a comment on pretentiousness. There is no lack of small pretensions we can look at and make fun of in good spirit. A man may not now aspire to climb Mr. Olympus, but he still wants to "get a good wife, to rear a good family, to establish himself in a good business, and to be respectable in council, academy, and church." When he works at any of these accomplishments a little too zealously and trips over his feet, he is subject for good-natured laughter.

One of the most amusing of postures, intimates Mr. Kerr, is that of the man who loves his misery over strongly. He does not want conditions to change. The image of his lostness—his isolation, his inability to communicate with his fellows, even his mortality—is dear to him. He has invested it with inverted, heroic qualities. Murray Schisgal has begun to satirize this concept, notably in the wry comedy *Luv*. Maybe out of this we shall begin to develop again at least one kind of large comedy appropriate to our age.

If the playgoer finds himself confused by the never resting whirl of cosmic inquiry, he usually has plenty to occupy his inquisitive mind in the more intimate problems of human behavior. A spectator, let us repeat, has a yen to crawl into the minds *as well as* the muscles of the individuals he is contemplating so he can sense out, test out, new viewpoints in a spirit of adventure—and thus, hopefully perhaps, improve his own approach to "stroking" his human companions. One such viewpoint, prompted by nothing much more than curiosity, may be interesting for historical reasons. A playgoer may take a special satisfaction in following the growing mind of a future president of the United States in the country youth depicted in *Abe Lincoln in Illinois*, or the developing thoughts of a future Queen of England in the frightened little girl shown in *Victoria Regina*. Another viewpoint may have an attraction because of its connection with an occupation or with an environment about which the playgoer has wished to know more. If he is particularly interested in the deliberations of soldiers under the stress of war he may seek out a production of *Paths of Glory*, *Journey's End*, or, in the context of men shut away from active fighting in a prisoners' camp, *Stalag 17*. If he wants military life suffused with comedy he can take *No Time for Sergeants*.

Generally more engaging than the purely informational attitudes are of course the psychological perspectives. Every playgoer, let us suggest again, seeks constantly for a fresh angle of vision on himself, his neighbors, and the world at large; he is stimulated when he assumes other people's viewpoints—even experimentally, perhaps very temporarily—to see if any of them can be made to fit his own questing nature. The advantage of doing this as a spectator in the playhouse over doing it as a reader in a library is that in the playhouse he can not only think about them rationally, but also inhabit them feelingly, and thus give them a fuller, more *living*, test. Even if the playgoer does not finally adopt any of the viewpoints he tries out this way, he is grateful for the opportunity to get acquainted with them. Each new viewpoint suggests another way of "stroking." The man who has experienced in one way or another many perspectives is much more knowledgeable, assured, comfortable (because flexible) in his transactions with his companions than he who has held steadily throughout the years to just one or two.

Roughly, there are as many general points of view as there are dramas; as many specific points of view as there are characters in those dramas. Some viewpoints are unique. Many more are rather similar. On the broadest level they can be distinguished as objective or subjective. A lot, the most common, are summed up in popular sayings:

"Fear has big eyes."

"The mills of the gods grind slowly."

"Hell hath no fury like a woman scorned."

"He who would pick roses must beware the thorns."

(If one wishes to examine illustrations of these commonplaces embodied in drama, he may turn to *Macbeth, Oedipus, Medea,* and *Much Ado about Nothing*.) The platitudes are described as "crystallizations of the folk wisdom of the human race"; it is interesting to see how much alike they are in different parts of the world. Here for instance is a Chinese aphorism:

"Man is the head of the family, woman the neck that turns that head."

There is something equivalent to this in every language on earth! Classic examples are: J. M. Barrie's *What Every Woman Knows,* Lillian Hellman's *The Little Foxes,* and *Macbeth.*

But the playgoer may not be satisfied only to have his convictions regarding human behavior comfortably or uncomfortably reaffirmed. He may like also to have some of them challenged. That is the way he grows in understanding.

A bird in the hand is worth two in a bush. Few people would disagree in general with this statement; one can assume that the individual who subscribes over strongly to this saying must be a conservative.

A rebel enters the scene. "I don't support that pale platitude," he says. "I want to reverse it." So he proposes, or falls in line with, a revised thought: *The wild thing in the bush is far more intriguing than a dozen tame things in your hand!* The artist who states this is an adventurer. A liberal playgoer may enjoy following his thought through an evening of vicarious living with a strong desire to see the inverted thought vindicated; as John Drinkwater did in his comedy, *Bird in Hand.*

Take another common saying: *'Tis love that makes the world go round.* A person with a comic turn of mind may wish to add some words to this: "Yes! And the prospect of a trip to Europe and a pretty home in the country may help love to spin the world a little faster!" Or a cynic will come along and insist that "the kind of love that exists between man and woman in some parts of America today tends to make the world go backwards!" Typically varied examples of the whirling world of love: Shakespeare's *Romeo and Juliet*, Anderson's *Elizabeth the Queen*, Kanin's *Born Yesterday*, Hellman's *Toys in the Attic*, O'Neill's *Long Day's Journey into Night*, and Albee's *Who's Afraid of Virginia Woolf?*

In another play there may be an entirely different individual, an idealist, who will argue strongly for the dynamic value of love, but qualified by the thought that the love which is finally effective between two people is that which spills beyond the confines of a home and embraces others in the community. The idealist may be so convinced of this that he will wish to spend his efforts through the length of a full evening's drama trying to prove the rightness of it. If the spectator agrees with the playwright he will go along with him—at least for tonight. Tomorow, with the action of the play dimming in his mind and finding himself affected by other pressures, he may change his belief back to the one he held before he went to the play. However, for a little while his view of humanity has been stretched by a more than ordinary feeling of generosity.

These statements of personal belief and the way they might be incorporated into plays are illustrations. There can be of course many other approaches—in certain instances, viewpoints never yet expressed in any aphorism. The plays of Bertolt Brecht, for example, are singularly free from any reference to platitudes. Brecht seems to have made a strong point of avoiding them. A prior expression is of course unimportant so long as the thought is clear and the playgoer can feel that he can get inside of it.

One of the greatest of contradictions today occurs between postures of gentleness and affection on one side and violence and rage on the other. At the moment, the second set of postures seems to be in the ascendance. The restless spirit of skepticism is abroad. The winds of cynicism blow across the land. Many of our younger authors see little they think they can write about except what pertains to pain, corruption, the cry of alienated men and women haunted by nightmares, the compulsive death wish. Certain playwrights appear to have an almost primitive desire to perform as witch doctors. The pervading influence in their kind of drama springs of course from the concepts of Antonin Artaud referred to in Chapter I.

Fed up with the stilted, sterile Boulevard (comparable to "Broadway") Theatre in France in the period after World War I, Antonin Artaud was determined to stage a revolt against it. Boulevard drama was characterized by its overlay of excessive civilization. "The theatre will never find itself again," Artaud declared in *The Theater and Its Double*,ᵏ . . . except by furnishing the spectator with the truthful precipitates of dreams, in which his taste for crime, his erotic obsessions, his savagery, his chimeras, his utopian sense of life and matter, even his cannabalism, pour out on a level not counterfeit and allusory, but interior."[2] So he turned back to early man. "All true culture," he believed, "relies upon the barbaric and primitive means of totemism whose savage, i.e., entirely spontaneous, life I wish to worship."[3] Artaud decreed that a scream of protest should be regarded as the theme of the new drama. Emotion, not thought, was to be the aim.

The present strength of the Theatre of Cruelty—meaning by "cruelty" the shock of rebellion rather than any excessive spilling of blood—is in its re-emphasis of the dramatic value of *sensation*, and of the kind of *physical movement* that is impelled by feeling rather than by intellect. As such it has exerted a strong influence on much of modern drama, especially the deliberately irrational phase of it. It has returned a measure of Dionysian excitement to the theatre. Its weakness lies in its trend toward directionlessness. Everything, say the rebels, must spring from the moment and it must create an effect just for that moment. Another limitation exists in its mistrust of words. Words are servants of the intellect. They are enemies of emotion. Words are a part of, a primary cause of, the inhibiting overlay of civilization. Therefore, words should be suppressed. Artaud once listed among the proposed items for production in his new playhouse in Paris: "Works from the Elizabethan theater [including Shakespeare] stripped of their text and retaining only the accouterments of period, situation, characters, and action."[4]

The greatest point for challenge, I feel, stands in the fact that while the Theatre of Cruelty is tremendously vigorous in attack, it seems to have small place in its plays for the feelings of love. Exercise is frenzied. Voices are shrill. Contact is by assault. Sex is sensual. Action destroys but never rebuilds. It laughs,

---

2. Antonin Artaud, *The Theater and Its Double*, trans. Mary Caroline Richards (New York: Grove Press, Inc., 1958), p. 92.
3. *Ibid.*, p. 10.
4. *Ibid.*, p. 100.

but never with joy. It has no tolerance for poetry. It is spiritually naked. It is ruthless. Its effect is strong but temporary—like needled beer's.

One scarcely needs to have pointed out to him that shadows in the theatre are not new. Plays that emphasize the darker sides of human nature have been performed in every age, and playgoers have gone to see them. One recalls readily such compelling nightmares as Euripides' *Medea*, Webster's *The Duchess of Malfi*, Shelly's *The Cenci*, Strindberg's *Ghost Sonata* and Wedekind's *Pandora's Box*. What distinguishes these compositions however is a magnitude of imagination and a grace of poetic expression—in greatest part verbal—that few of the modern dramas of ruthlessness now possess.

But by and large the view that the average playgoer[5] finally seeks most of the time, I think, is not one that is *pointedly* social, psychiatric, or moralistic, but what is concerned with the playing of simple games of human coexistence. More often than not their setting is domestic. The subject usually turns out to be a problem of getting together (occasionally, separating), and the motivating forces behind the actions to be a love and a hate. There may be implications of other issues, but they are not predominant. A few of these dramas and comedies are very good; many are weak. They all indicate, however, a prevailing taste.

Plays infected with the kind of thinking referred to still occupy most of the Broadway theatres and community playhouses each season and fill most of the television sets in people's homes every night. One thinks readily of such pieces as *The Moon Is Blue, Born Yesterday, Any Wednesday, Barefoot in the Park*. Dr. Eric Berne certainly had no intention of aiming *Games People Play* at the theatre (it was meant to be a guide for mental-health specialists), but one cannot read it without recognizing in it the themes of scores of dramatic entertainments one has seen. The names that Dr. Berne has given his games could serve, with only minor alterations, as titles for plays:

5. See p. viii.

"Sweethearts," "Kick Me," "Now See What You Made Me Do!" "Let's You and Him Fight," "The Stocking Game," "How Do We Get Out of Here?" "Let's Pull a Fast One on Joey," "They'll Be Glad They Knew Me," "Now I've Got You You Son of a Bitch"—there are over a hundred of them.

Most games acted out on the stage are obvious, familiar, and open. Some few are covered with an intellectual veil which invites the observer to do a bit of guessing. These are the mind-teasers. The playwright who is the most adept at writing these puzzles—games, as it were, within games—is, of course, Luigi Pirandello. A younger author who is fast catching up on him is Harold Pinter. There are others. Some of their works of mystification are quite seductive; some remain so misty that one is tempted sometimes to question whether there is actually much to seek under the veil.

However these "coexistent" dramas are developed, nearly all of them are based on three playgoer-based premises: (1) human affection is normal, desirable but illusive; (2) personal loneliness is normal, undesirable but all too prevailing; and (3) something should be done about both of them!

VI. A Sense of Illumination—

ALL TOGETHER

The playgoer demands that the product he views on the stage have good sense not only in its parts but also in its entirety. He asks that it all add up to something meaningful. If the end is chaos, it must be at least a meaningful chaos! And he wants the conclusion to be arrived at without fits and starts. If he is a sentimentalist, he may ask for an ending affected by a sense of poetic justice with the protagonist of righteousness triumphant and the villain punished. If he is a man less insistent on the inherent invincibility of moral force, he may demand another kind of poetic ingredient. That is what might be called "poetic logic." This is an essential reasonableness—a recognition that a bid for a certain kind of response from the audience in one part of the drama will be supported by a bid for an equivalent and related response in another. In spite of the label, all of the more successful of the modern "irrational plays" possess a core of reasonableness in them. They are motivated by a set purpose and proceed to the fulfillment of this.

A failure with respect to poetic logic can be seen very clearly in the all-too-common beginning script of the young playwright who asks his audience to weep bitterly with him over the sad fate of his hero who wishes to be an author but finds that he has to go to work for his father in the front office of a steel mill—when nothing whatsoever has been established about the put-upon boy's ever having shown a shred of literary talent to begin with! Or in the other frequent script which demands grief because a wonderful princess-heroine, in love with a boy in an acting school, allows herself to become pregnant right at the moment the young man is ready to desert her to take his first small role in "stock"—without ever having established what there was in him to make him her one-in-a-thousand choice in the first place! Perhaps actually now, the audience will feel she is lucky to be rid of him! That's too bad for the author.

At the close of the evening a spectator likes to be able to sum up his revealing experiences in a simple thought. Or if not in a thought, at least in a feeling. He may not be able to verbalize it exactly, but he should have a fairly compact sense of it. If he has just seen an able performance of A *Streetcar Named Desire*, the trend of his thinking might very well have something to do with the tragic futility of trying to recapture a past glory. The play is a complicated one and other playgoers, looking more to Stella or to Stanley than to Blanche, might extract a different kind of summary thought. That would not matter much, because Tennessee Williams has written what all will agree is a unified play, and it can be viewed without confusion from several different angles, each of which taken singly can be completely valid, and so intellectually and emotionally satisfying.

The human summation can be thoroughly good and yet have a tone which is not the least bit solemn. The comedies are among the most potent of comment makers. Think of the high-spirited compositions of Bernard Shaw. Think of the thought which springs out of Rodgers and Hammerstein's *South Pacific*: "Love can be, and often is, international." The conclusion for *Oklahoma* might be just, "The most delectable girl in the world is not so much one who is pretty—though that helps—as one with spirit!" Or the thought might be even simpler than that: "The most important thing to do on a beautiful morning is to sing!" We could guess that a good over-all idea for *My Fair Lady* would be, "You can't create a thing of loveliness—especially if that thing is a woman—and then leave it out in the cold!" To say that such a thought is obvious and that one need not go to the theatre to discover it is beside the point because it fails to recognize the fundamental fact: the playhouse is not a place for discovery but for rediscovery—rediscovery, expanded, made clear, vivid, lively, and feelingful by the aid of dramatic action.

Let us say once again, the one really central demand of the spectator in the playhouse is that his experience there shall give him a heightened sense of being alive. He can feel alive without having his mind operate at fever pitch, it is true. His desire for a clarification of the confusion of human nature is not always paramount. But rarely is he happy if it is ignored entirely. Even the most sophisticated playgoer likes an occasion to take his hair down and romp, as it were, without a serious thought in his head. However, he cannot take the purely physical type of stimulation very long without asking for some spur for his mind. Since his participation in the theatre is so eminently personal, involving finally as it does every part of his intellectual as well as physical nature, he needs to be assured of the continuing existence of meaningful human relationships. He wants to see the verification of this in images which he can see, hear and, by imagination, inhabit as well.

One of the chief problems the craftsman faces as he constructs his characters is keeping them in the proper balance. The greatest difficulty that will be encountered is balancing the opposing figures.

No story is stronger than its hero. No hero is stronger than his villain. Just about everything that has been said so far about the three-dimensional character of the head man in the dramatic story is equally valid when applied to his opponent. The unsympathetic figure will have the darker qualities, of course. In order to make the antagonist have an interesting play of dimensions, the author may have to endow him with certain admirable qualities, also. The antagonist may be marked by a surface charm. Or he may show a very genuine love for his wife. Or he may display an enviable talent for witty conversation. But taken in the whole breadth and depth of his character, the antagonist does not elicit love. He is the *challenger of the protagonist*; as such he belongs to the category of darkness.

This is the classical conception of the duality of hero and opponent. However, the patterns of drama do not always conform to it neatly. In the performance of a well-composed play the protagonist usually stands out clearly. This is not always true of his opposite. Take a production of *Hamlet* or *Othello*; in it, the playgoer can find the antagonist without difficulty. But where does one look for him in *Macbeth?* The hero is there prominently. He is not wholly an admirable character, it is true; he is greedy and cowardly. Yet he does hold resolutely before him an image of what he believes to be his rightful status in Scotland. This we can understand. He is striving for honor. With this we can sympathize; we hope that he will win what he wants —not through the means he seems mistakenly to be using, but somehow. Macbeth is surely the protagonist of his drama.

But who is his opponent? In this case the spectator will probably find him in a force rather than in a person. Macbeth very evidently runs into something with which he has to struggle. What is it? Is it a spirit world? Perhaps it is the belief (held by the people of Shakespeare's England) in the sacredness of the king's person. Macbeth's violation of this principle causes his tragic defeat. In effect, the antagonist wins. He is not a visible being. Yet—this is important—he is not permitted to be wholly unsubstantial either. The spectator sees his face in the form of Duncan, then in the wraith of Banquo, and finally in the avenging figure of Macduff. So the antagonist here *is* something more than just spirit.

A modern puzzler is Shaw's *Candida*. The protagonist is certainly Marchbanks. The play is named for the woman in the story. She is not the initiator of action, so she cannot rightfully be regarded as heroine. A part of her does resist the advances of Marchbanks. So one might regard that aspect of Candida as the antagonist. The opposition to the poet's achievement of his desire is the older woman's reluctance to say "yes" when he proposes. So the opposition—it would be a mistake to call it "villain" —is in essence an unseen spirit of mature wisdom, speaking through the voice of a fleshly woman. The spectator does not analyze all this intellectually. What he does sense is the existence of an issue between two contrary forces precipitating a dramatic struggle which ends in a defeat—or in a victory (depending on how one wishes to view the outcome). *And the opposing forces can be seen and heard in the forms of sensible imagery.* It should be recognized that a good many modern plays, such as the plays of Samuel Beckett, deliberately avoid the setting up of personalized heroes and villains. In them the protagonist is just Man, and the antagonist is a mindless and heartless force of the universe.

Any dealing with a theatre game inevitably calls attention to its parts, moment by moment. But, if the involvment is successful, it compels the attention also to something bigger than the segments. The play in the playhouse reflects the desires and the efforts of human living broadly as well as narrowly; the spectator who becomes engaged by imagination in the progress of staged action wants to see it so arranged as to let him look back over it at the end with a satisfying feeling of cumulative perspective. Physically, intellectually, and spiritually the action has grown, block by block, like living architecture, into a unity; it produces now one final dramatic experience.

There are works shown on the stage today that do not, unfortunately, lead to this sense of final arrival. They tend to be fragments only, mental explorations, technical etudes, small-scale emotional exercises. As such they have their values. But they cannot give a complete satisfaction to the playgoer because they cannot move him as a singly integrated and directed organism.

One of the greatest of unifying influences is of course a cultural frame of reference. This starts with the assumption that the spectator's domestic, social, national, and international thinking has been conditioned through the years by what he has heard, seen, and talked about among the people with whom he has grown up. It includes the assumption also that the spectator's upbringing has given him feelings about certain religious tenets, about moral codes, about prejudices, about politics, about the themes of literature and the arts. Add to this what he has been exposed to in the way of the folk behavior, folk beliefs, and even the folk stories and folk music of his neighborhood. Any aspect of these serves as a ground on which the artist can build his work with the knowledge that a foundation for unity already exists. The rebel artist thinks he can ignore this kind of ground; when he does he inevitably comes a cropper.

Typical examples of the traditional cultural starting points are the Judaeo-Christian philosophy of the worth of the individual, the Greek attitude on the importance of reason, the pagan concept of fertility and of the image of the dying and resurrected king of nature, the cult of the warrior chief, the belief in the efficacy of the golden rule, the rightness of the American constitution, Freudian concepts, evolution.

Another of the most potent groups of influence on patterns of thinking comes from our treasury of familiar stories: the classical myths, the fairy tales of childhood, the Biblical narratives. Who does not think and talk about the *hubris* of Agamemnon, the evil effect of the Oedipus complex, and the murderous jealously of Medea; who is unaffected by the emotional relationships of Electra and her brother Orestes, of the conflicting attitudes of Antigone and King Creon, and the loyalty of Ulysses and his faithful Penelope? Who has been able to forget the youthful courage of Jack with his beanstalk, and the wonderful rise of Cinderella from her ashes? Is there anyone whose heart has ceased to be stirred by the stories of the Ugly Duckling, the Sleeping Beauty, Beauty and the Beast, Bluebeard, and Puss in Boots? The symbolical implications of these tales are far-reaching; they influence our adult as well as our childhood thinking. Even more pervasive with regard to both our feeling and thoughtful attitudes are the Biblical stories of David who conquered Goliath, Joseph who resisted Potiphar's wife, David who yearned after lovely Bathsheba, Joshua who trumpeted down the walls of Jericho, and—in a different, more spiritual context—the account of Jacob who struggled for his soul with the angel. Stories from the life of Jesus influence the thoughts of both religious and nonreligious people.

The author who regards these backgrounds may personally have small fondness for any of them. He may want to get away from them as fast as he can. But he cannot ignore their existence. One of the tenets or one of the stories will serve one artist as a parallel. For another artist, it will be a reference for a disagreement. Either way, it serves a useful purpose; it provides a focal point for departure and so promotes a unifying effect.

Among the most powerful of the pervading tenets of Western man are the Ten Commandments, particularly these:

Thou shalt not kill.

Thou shalt not steal.

Thou shalt not bear false witness.

Thou shalt not covet thy neighbor's wife.

The advantage the traditional attitudes, the common tales, and the generally accepted, or "moral," rules of conduct have is that they carry with them certain emotional mind-sets which affect the spectator's outlook. Again let us say, before the play ever begins, the playwright who proposes to use one of them as a theme for his drama need not feel that he has permanently to be bound by it; he can show how desirable may be a certain modification of it, or twist it into comedy or satire, and perhaps end up with a new and totally radical conclusion. However, the fact that he *started* with a commonplace as a point of departure gives him a chance to pull the minds of his audience together at one thought before he starts to lead them off on his own unique adventure.

Yet another device for unity is the frame of a well-known ritual, such as the religious ceremonial of wedding, baptism, or funeral. Many plays have exploited the images of Christmas Eve. Others have used the forms associated with the Easter sunrise service. One of the most potent of the pagan rituals also has been used time without number: the resurrection in spring of the king of fertility. Another ritual is the rite of sacrifice. There are a number of rites associated with the death of criminals, and still others with the triumphant return of the warrior hero. For the dramatists who wish to deal with murder and with the darker obsessions of the mind there is an abundance of ready-made ceremonials connected with witchcraft and with the exorcising of devils.

An absolute requisite for unity is of course a consistency of style. Style begins with a singleness of viewpoint. It bears witness to the fact that the author started with something either serious or comic he wanted to say and did not change his mind in the middle of his composition. It shows that the playwright, the director, and the actors—*all* of them—knew at the beginning of rehearsals just what this was and had a firm agreement among themselves to abide by it.

Style means a singleness of manner or mode—realistic, abstract, suggestive, symbolical, prose, poetical, burlesque, or something else—and sticking to this. Unity of style in this sense does not imply a stodgy type of unimaginative conformity; when a play does use variety—such as may be required, for instance, in the staging of one of the plays by Bertolt Brecht—it maintains a balanced consistency. When a performance of this kind begins, the audience is tipped off to the fact that what is to be presented will be given in a way involving a little more playfulness than usual. There will be some prose, some poetry, some dancing, and some singing. If the spectator can feel behind all this fantastic motion and sound a strong thread of single thought, he will relax and allow himself to move flexibly with the show.

The games that exploit contrasts of experience played by men, women, and children of the everyday, nontheatrical world are infinitely varied. Since the art of the playmaking world must be based on the forms of an active world, if it is to seem true, the simulations have to be as varied as those they strive to represent. There will be some redesigning to serve the purposes of intensity, focus, and the limitations on the time an observer can be persuaded to remain in his seat. But, *basically*, the shapes of gaming adventures in the theatre have to be reminiscent of those experienced outside; there cannot be restrictions on this. A playgoer tends to resent the sight of a play constructed in accordance with an obviously technical formula. The synthetic work may have a surface glitter but it rings no bells in the memory of the playgoer's senses and heart, and to his mind it recalls nothing of what is natural to his own way of playing himself through life. Here is the reason for the ineffectiveness of so many of the so-called "well-made" dramas of both the past and the present.

But if we admit that formula makes for weakness in theatre, we cannot assume consequently that drama can be free from all rules. Every art has to have rules. The rules of the theatre spring quite properly from the laws of nature, and they can be found in the wholly-human, inevitably present desires of the playgoer uninstructed in how he *should* respond. The playgoer enjoys his whole experience on two levels: his participation in the action of the play, and his recognition of the skills of the play-craftsmen (playwright, actors, designers, the several environmental artists, and the co-ordinating director) who present it.

The necessity of a conclusion is sometimes questioned today. It is my firm conviction, however, that dramatic rules based on a universal concept of games cannot avoid including the image of a goal. The playhouse experience that omits it (what we have designated as a *no-plot scene* as distinguished from a *conventional play*) may be interesting, but it is seldom deeply moving. It is not *fully* dramatic.

The following chapter will analyze the character of the playgoer's fulfillment in a play's conclusion.

Attaining a Goal

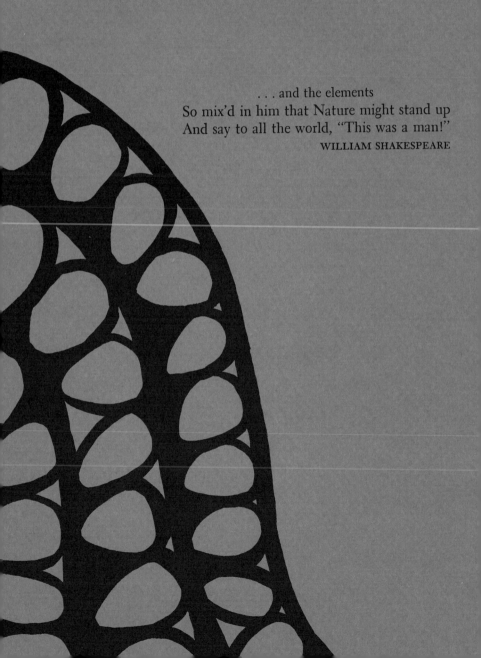

. . . and the elements
So mix'd in him that Nature might stand up
And say to all the world, "This was a man!"
WILLIAM SHAKESPEARE

VII. A SENSE OF
FULFILLMENT

"The presence of an aim or a goal gives meaning to an activity," observe Sapora and Mitchell. "It is the goal that gives play value to activities, and the measure of the play value is found in the intensity with which the goal is sought." Dr. Berne sees the outcome of a game played all the way through as being "dramatic." The attainment of some kind of goal is the *characteristic ending* of the playgoer's adventure in the playhouse.

If the curtain on the play currently occupying the theatre on South Delaney Street goes up tonight at 8:30, it should come down for the first intermission at about 9:20. If any spectator wishes to go home at this time, he can simply walk out the door, get into his car in the parking lot, and be on his way. Those who remain are presumably sufficiently intrigued by the question of the future events in the story they have come to participate in to want to have a peek at the second act.

At about 10:15 there will be a second intermission. Here is another opportunity for departure. Probably, if the play is any good, none of the patrons will wish to go away then. Since the members of the audience have already sat patiently in their seats for over an hour and a half watching the scenes go by one after another, they will feel they would be cheating themselves if they did not wait a little longer for the ending. The spectators want to see, and have a share in, the conclusion of the story. They want the payoff for their evening's attendance at the playhouse.

What that will be will depend, of course, on the nature of the drama the spectators have allowed themselves to be engaged in; each play rightly presents its own kind of reward. In general, what the playgoer is waiting for can be described as a final moment that serves as a backward, emotion-filled view on all the asking, striving, searching, wanting, failing, and renewed trying to get somewhere, or to discover something, in the past two and a half hours—a moment that casts a glow on this past experience and gives it meaning. It may express itself in a speech. What is more likely is that it will take the form of an act—such as a smile, a frown, the slam of a door, or just a handshake, or even a walking to the window to look far off to an imaginary presence beyond the horizon. It may be a sigh or a laugh. The speech or the act is not properly the payoff itself. It is what the speech or act *implies* now in retrospect about the play as a whole; and, also in anticipation about the protagonist's future in the light of the experience just seen.

A very young child plays solely for the fun of playing. Perhaps the game in which he engages himself does involve a momentary desire to "beat out" an opponent. But that is secondary. The principal pleasure he derives from his exercise is what he feels about his body and mind in motion. An older person plays in part for the same pleasure—but usually also for something else. This added thing is an attainment. The thing he wants to feel he will have, if he plays his game right, is an object or state of being that will fill out—perhaps only in happy imagination and lasting no longer than a moment—a spot of incompleteness in his command of life. The payoff then is that feeling of fulfillment. It is both the perspective just referred to and that which gives the perspective a present substance. Woe to the playcraftsman if the playgoer does not get this!

What each of us is desperately hungry for, let us repeat, is a sense of being *on top* of life rather than *under it*. Through imagination, a man can feel that he is standing on a summit from which he looks down on a segment of existence and knows that he not only sees it, but also controls it, in effect possesses it. But we need trained image-makers and guides to make us reach the summit. There are not many of them. Those who can lead us to the point of pleasurable perspective are the artists.

In his perceptive book, *Man's Search for Himself*, the psychologist Rollo May makes an interesting observation: "It is very easy to get an audience these days if one preaches against conceit and pride in one's self, for most people feel so empty and convinced of their lack of worth anyway that they readily agree that the one who is condemning them must be right." The special phenomenon of the middle years of the twentieth century is the existence of the "hollow man." Throughout his treatise, Dr. May refers to human emptiness. "I mean not only that many people do not know what they want; they often do not have any clear idea of what they feel. When they talk about lack of autonomy, or lament their inability to make decisions—difficulties which are present in all decades—it soon becomes evident that their underlying problem is that they have no definite experience of their own desires or wants."[1]

The prime cause of the pathological indefinitiveness is, of course, related to developments of our times; the moving of the human image into the figure of the machine, and the fading of the concept of individualism into the faceless, rootless, drifting crowd. Man today still seeks to exert himself. However, he can no longer see clearly how he should do it because he has no real consciousness of what his particular personal resources are. He has lost his sense of uniqueness. He is hollow.

The contrary state is integration. There are two ways in which a human being can arrive at this happy condition. One is to attach himself by imagination to a separate identity which already exerts the directed strength the hungry man yearns for. The other, and much harder way, is to build that strength in himself. In a contemplation of these choices, tradition tends to pit a religious myth against art. (The religious attitude referred to here is the conservative, of course, not the liberal.) The attitude of a man who views some god as being alone creative leads him to stress his own powerlessness. The artist, on the other hand, thinks and works with the concept of creativity lodged in his own being. It may have been derived from divinity,

1. Rollo May, *Man's Search for Himself* (New York: W. W. Norton and Company, 1953), pp. 98, 14.

but it now operates in him. *He must think this way; if he ever sensed himself as being uncreative in the presence of other forces superior to himself, he could no longer see himself as a Maker. He would be a Recorder only; he would not initiate.* The creator has to be a self-starter. Deep inside, everyman—artist or layman—is hungry for the power to *begin* things. Here is how a work of true art puts its mark on the observer: it leads him through participation in the artist's action to feel the glow of creativeness. It makes him feel in himself the initiative strength of the artist—and, beyond the artist, in the human creature the artist creates.

In *The World, the Arts, and the Artist,* the philosopher Irwin Edman draws his conception of the man in whose creativity the observer has a desire in imagination to participate. The theme of art, says Edman, is properly "the whole of experience; its materials and its theatre the whole of life." Then, "The artist when he ceases to be merely a gifted and trifling craftsman turns out to be in his choice of themes, in his very selection of materials, in his total and residual effect, a commentator on life and in his immediate and imaginative way a philosopher." His power, his posture of confidence and command, are possessions in which the spectator longs to share.

From a contrasting position, Dr. May refers to the crowds which are attracted to the preacher talking of the evils of pride. The preacher may be in the pulpit; he may be in the classroom; he may be on a political platform. He properly has little place in the theatre. The dramatic artist deals, like the preacher, with the pain experienced by the hollow people, but he does it in a way reversed from the other. He accepts it as being his function to show through art a way (not *away from*) *toward* pride in oneself and in the energy that springs from this. He may point with anger to present imperfections—imperfections which he thinks should be removed. Beyond these is the image of the fundamental self that the playgoer can, and should, respect.

Both the preacher and the dramatist start with the same premise: the human state of incompleteness. Human nature is associative; separation is unnatural. We are informed that in some societies people have been killed by being psychologically isolated from their fellows. Theatre exists to combat loneliness. It does so by making the playgoer feel, not *attached* to strength like the theistic man, but *integrated* like the artist. It gives him an identity.

A principal means for acquiring this feeling of identity for the playgoer who wants it is an active union with (not an inert attachment to) an image of vitality which moves and talks, makes choices, exerts its will—a living figure which has the wonderful qualities of fullness, positiveness, being a *personality which has to be reckoned with*. If this personality is vigorous enough, if it seems in some way really to "have life by the tail," the spectator will not only watch it with pleasure, he will also by imagination, become a part of its spirit and of its body and mind and so feel its strength.

What phase of the role will draw the greatest participation will depend on the particular potentialities of the spectator. One observer will be influenced by qualities of physical bravery, another by moral courage, still another by a capacity for intellectual insight. The attractive aspect may not be forcefully mobile, or moral, or loving. It may be a very quiet talent, for example, a power to think incisively about a subject concerning which the observer himself is passionately interested. In every case what invites union will be a sense of physical vitality or of intellectual perceptiveness that is ordered for maximum effect. Attaining this sense in depth will go a long way toward removing that feeling of incompleteness that the spectator had before he came to the theatre.

However, the sense of having attained in one's nature a greater sense of vitality and perceptiveness is only partly fulfilling. Feeling that one has the ability to live and to know gives one a feeling of well-being, but a limited one. Vitality and perceptiveness are means not ends. They bring to the spectator with an ambitious mind a complete satisfaction only when they open doors to a state of commitment to something beyond the present scene. The hollow man may be vigorous and he may be bright; he is still a hollow man until he has an idea which gives his vitality and brightness a direction for movement.

What the idea should be has been suggested by a very practical novelist and playwright, Somerset Maugham who, though he was not able to be completely an idealist himself, clearly saw the importance of something to cherish. In *The Summing Up*, he declares: "The value of art, like the value of the Mystic Way, lies in its effects. If it can give only pleasure, however spiritual that pleasure may be, it is of no great consequence or at least of no more consequence than a dozen oysters and a pint of Montrachet. . . . Art, if it is to be reckoned with as one of the great values of life, must teach man humility, tolerance, wisdom, and magnaminity. The value of art is not beauty but right action."[2] In the theatre each playmaker and each playgoer have to decide between them what that action is; but it is the playmaker who by intimation suggests it.

The great plays of the past have all been works dominated by strong characters eminently committed to something they wanted and were determined to get. Oedipus wants to find what is causing the plague in Thebes. He is determined to find it and eradicate it even if this means the destruction of himself. Macbeth wills himself to kingship. Hamlet wills a change of the forces responsible for his father's death. Faust wants knowledge; he wants it so much that he is willing to sell his soul to the Devil to get that knowledge. In our day Eugene O'Neill has created several personalities which have similar purposes: to find a better form of life beyond the horizon, to learn the meaning of self, to discover a base for life. Arthur Miller and Edward Albee are doing the same thing. The dramatic men and women in the plays of Bernard Shaw, Maxwell Anderson, Tennessee Williams, Paul Green, William Inge, Archibald MacLeish, John Osborne, Robert Bolt and of most of the other leading authors of our

2. W. Somerset Maugham, *The Summing Up* (New York: Pocket Books, 1967), p. 224.

time—even the strident rebels—have been searchers with definite goals, all related to the purpose of a productive self-realization in a form of action that they felt was important. If the action seems in retrospect to be worthy, the player will be affected by it, if unworthy, he will note how it went wrong. That too can be rewarding.

The spectator who plays along by imagination with an artist may not always be wholly agreeable about every aspect of the staged personalities with whom he has been drawn to a union in his mind; however, there is no question about his attitude toward their qualities of energy, action, and tenacity of purpose. With *these* aspects of human nature the spectator will be eager to unite himself absolutely anytime.

There is little sense of achievement if the playgoer finds himself associating by imagination through a long evening with a figure having no feeling of uniqueness, no convictions, no will; who communicates with no one outside of himself. His actions—insofar as they may be regarded as actions at all—and his words (they often are only grunts) may be a faithful transcription of the readily observable 90 per cent of human nature in every man. But as we have stated before, that is not why the general, normally healthy spectator dresses himself up to go to the theatre. What he hopes to find there is a reflection of that 10 per cent part of himself that he cherishes, so clarified and developed that by a re-experiencing of its true nature in the environment of the playhouse he can feel the superior, selected part of himself become for a while the whole of him!

Not everyone who goes to the theatre wants this kind of fulfillment. I believe, however, it is what most playgoers are looking for—in one way or another. Not the "cultural," the ever-questioning elite perhaps, but those whom we tend to refer to as "average" spectators.

One of the compelling reasons why the selective part of the human individual is sometimes rejected in modern writing is that it is affected by conscious daydreaming. Some dramatists who question the value of over-active sentiment believe this must be regarded as a false element—it is a part which has been grafted onto the essential man. It is unrealistic, untrue. Where, then, do we search for the truth of man? In that which exists in his subconscious? The author who is interested in "purity" is inclined to say "yes"! Asked for his recommendation on how to achieve a revelation of this in art, he replies: "Let us take a piece of the deep-lying urges, bring it, raw, hot, and bleeding to the surface and place it swiftly, without the corrupting effect of contemplation, on canvas, or on paper, or on the stage. There we can see the *real thing,* unaffected by the seductive influence of thoughts about appropriateness or the desire to conform to social or artistic conventions."

What does the spectator actually see in this "pure" object? Most frequently a very familiar image of violence, sexuality, loneliness, or fear. What usually comes out of the inner reaches of a person is basically primitive. And lo and behold, when it is revealed to the light of day it turns out to be very much like what has been dredged out of other people's subconscious! When this piece of inner stuff is recorded in the form of color, line, or words, it is stereotype. The truth that has been achieved is not very startling. It can be summed up simply in a commonplace statement that all human creatures are fundamentally brute beings. About the only thing that can be done about this thought is to try to express it in a new way.

The typical playgoer, since he is always painfully aware of the forces which war against each other in the evolution of a human self, is seldom very deeply or for very long intrigued by disintegration. The only time in which he can really enjoy the denigration of a man or woman's personality is when it is done so brilliantly that the playgoer can separate himself emotionally from the quivering figure being cut apart and identify himself with the mind of the critic-dramatist who is officiating at the dissection. Even this attitude is, in an oblique way, positive since the spectator is uniting himself with the superior acuity of the dissecting genius. The Devil of Destruction, whom we despise, can sometimes be, for short periods of time, tremendously fascinating.

This we must concede. It is the Angel of Life, however, who is the more continuously sustaining.

The most valuable commodity of the theatre is and always will be human character; it cannot be handled casually. The ablest artist is he who starts with a devotion to the most vital elements of it and leads the spectator to a feeling of union with them.

Every man, woman, and child beyond the age of infancy, cherishes in his mind the image of an ideal state. In this imaginary existence he exercises fully all his talents with no restraint, he feels completely secure, he commands all the affection of his fellow creatures, and he looks forward to an even greater possession of and control over those things which make life good.

The typical spectator (even the intellectualist) *does* enter the house of drama as a daydreamer. He may not wish to admit it, but daydreaming is a continuing part of him. He cannot help it. No amount of sophistication will relieve him from wanting something. It may be a possession; another person's companionship, being in on a new creative enterprise, wealth, position, the center of a crowd's admiring attention, someone's love. It may be, on the other hand, not so much the acquisition of something he does not have as the preservation of something of value which he does have and now feels in danger of losing: the unity of his family, the continuing affection of his wife, the loyalty of his friend, a moral or religious conviction, his self respect. He is quite aware that the theatre cannot give him actually either a possession or a preservation of possession, but he is impelled by desire to play the game of seeing a dream worked out *as if it were something worthy of being dealt with*. It is quite possible that the particular dream he sees proposed on the stage will not match what he is longing for outside this theatre at this time, but the very act of being involved in someone else's desires and the fulfillment of them will, if they are well presented, give him a pleasurable feeling of emotional exercise. It will momentarily, at least, relieve the pain of his own wants outside the playhouse.

And it can do more. The practice of the mind and muscles exerted in the game of striving can give one a feeling of purposeful strength that will stay with one a long time.

Rosalind wants Orlando, and she bends every effort by wile to get him. Faust wants knowledge; he wants it so much he is willing to sell the most precious part of himself for it. The Good Woman of Setzuan wants to be an effective citizen. The Madwoman of Chaillot wants the power to effect the destruction of ugliness in Paris, and she organizes a whole band of men and women to drive the ugliness into the underground sewers. On the other hand, there are the personalities who are trying, not to get, but to save. Richard II loves the state of kingship; he tries to retain it. The Merchant of Venice attempts to preserve his pound of flesh. Berenger in *Rhinoceros* strives to safeguard his self independence. Hedda Gabler seeks desperately to keep her sense of control over the lives of people more creative than she. The Caretaker in Harold Pinter's play wants to stay in his newfound home. The playgoer in a playful (albeit also quite serious) mood enters into the enactment of such people's efforts to achieve what they desire and, by reason of this gameful participation, feels a sort of refreshment with respect to his own desires.

Those dramas which appeal most directly to the spectator's ready inclination to participate are the ones which deal with the universal subjects of sexual passion, human companionship, the desire for power over other people, and the prevention of a loss of love, loyalty, or self respect. Complementing these are a host of less physically active, more contemplative, works which deal with mental attitudes. These are the philosophical mood pieces. An outstanding example is Eugene O'Neill's *Long Day's Journey into Night*. Another is his *The Iceman Cometh*. The principals of this play are derelicts in a bar, sodden, essentially hopeless individuals, each of whom has however a little dream which he still cherishes lovingly. The dream is about a piece of redeeming action he will undertake some day—when the conditions are just right—which will restore his own and his fellows' respect for him, and will prove to the world that he is indeed a man of worth. The dream is placed, as it were, in a jewel box for safekeeping and the possessor of it actually wants it to remain there. The character who in a brief moment of mistaken enthusiasm persuades his friends to remove the dreams from their cotton wrappings succeeds only in showing the worthlessness of the dreams and thereby destroys the last remnants of their owners' happiness.

The spectator who observes this play may gain a wry satisfaction in getting a new look at the little illusion he has been treasuring in his own jewel box. More likely he will see, with the help of the playwright, something besides—the futility of shutting up in one's soul a dream which is left too long unexercised, and a scrap of new respect for his own stumbling efforts to keep plugging along toward the more moderate goals that can be realized—so, in a way, his vision is clarified and he feels a bit of pleasurable attainment in the achievement.

In this somewhat lengthy description of the positive approach to the art of effective playmanship, it should be apparent in what directions my own convictions happen to move. In my observation the dramatic artist, however sharp his mind is, works himself into a dead end unless he gives respect to his playgoer's desire for a satisfying close to his night's adventures in the playhouse. The spectator cannot, must not, leave either confused or depressed. (A feeling of puzzlement is a form of depression.) This is emphatically not a question of morality or of abstract aesthetics. It involves nothing more than the nature of the playhouse to which people come always for some experience of *refreshment*. Of course, the kind of refreshment desired varies with the audience. One group inclined inherently to optimistic viewpoints likes a certain kind of fulfillment—the bright kind. I think that it is utterly unfair to label this sort of body "childlike" or "middle-class," because there are plenty of sophisticates who support happy endings, maybe not all of the time, but at least a part of the time.

There is also the opposite type of audience, the one so fundamentally obsessed by the astringent feeling of pain that it cannot even play at having an escape from it. Strange as it may seem, I believe that it is quite possible for it too to experience a refreshment. The chief sting of pain comes from a feeling that it is buried. Theatre performs one of its most valuable functions when it pulls the inward agonies to the surface where they can be seen for what they really are. Where the causes can be examined, where the hurts can be compared, where they can be related to contrary conditions of hope and health and be thereby clarified. Just the act of verbalizing the pains helps to purge them. The playgoer who goes through this experience may never attain a feeling of joy, but he does arrive at a feeling of stimulation by way of the new perspective. One of the most pleasurable (refreshing) experiences one can have, it seems, is to feel that one has achieved a clearer eyesight. One has assumed the role of a wiseman, even if one must play it with a mask of tears.

To summarize, the thing the craftsman is dealing with in the theatre is characteristically that sense of achievement we have when we can imagine ourselves to be *possessors*, particularly *power-affected possessors*. What we willfully make believe we have at such a moment may be material wealth. More often it is something much more fundamental: that which gives us a feeling of meaningful relatedness to other active human beings; or of holding in our grasp a physical, mental, or spiritual implement for sustaining or extending our present state of well-being; or of having the assurance of a place in a universe which has threatened to divest itself of us—of the ownership of anything which helps us to resist the insidious influence of the Great Darkness around us.

What "possession" means in this context is the ability to assert to ourselves: "This creature which stands in these shoes is *I*. These human associations, these physical and these spiritual pertinences, are *mine*. They were struggled for and won by *my efforts*. These thoughts which I think spring from a mind that belongs *to me* and constitute thereby a unique world of action in which my will is still dominant."

Play-acting? Yes. But a kind of play-acting that embraces an inward reality demanding expression—in the theatre.

Double Game

Were you thinking that those were the words,
    those upright lines? those curves, angles, dots?
No, those are not the words—the substantial
    words are in the ground and sea,
They are in the air—they are in you. . . .
All merges toward the presentation
    of the unspoken meanings of the earth!
Toward him who sings the songs
    of the Body and of the truths of the earth,
Toward him who makes dictionaries
    of words that print cannot touch.

WALT WHITMAN

VIII. OPPORTUNITIES
AND RESPONSIBILITIES

The double game of theatre goes forward, as we have noted, on two levels. On the first, the playgoer engages himself by imagination sensuously and intellectually with the dramatic characters he watches on the stage. On the second, he interacts with the artist as playmaker (the man who creates the play in which the playgoer is immersing himself).

The two phases of the complicated game overlap at so many points that an outside observer often has difficulty in seeing where one phase ends and the other begins. The performer while performing will be only partially conscious of their separateness, and the fully-engaged spectator may never think of their differences at all. But the two phases do exist, and both must be considered.

The part of the game involving the playgoer's participation in the drama has already been covered pretty thoroughly in this book; the second phase only to a limited extent. The following pages contain a few additional suggestions regarding the playwright and performer's opportunities and responsibilities in regard to the second phase.

The most effective method that can be devised for perking up a playgoer's sensory faculties is, as we have suggested, to confront him with a series of stimuli planned in a pattern of variety. The key factor is *change*. Drama has been defined as the art of creating surprises under a condition of control. The little surprises build up to the big surprise. So there is suspense—waiting for the next surprise, which will probably be a little one but may be a big one. The ingredient in the situation which makes surprise produce its peculiar effect is the quality of difference which something present has from something that preceded it. The spectator has adjusted himself to see, to think, to feel, and by imagination to act in one direction and finds himself suddenly called upon to see, to think, to feel, and to act in another. If the pattern of changes is well arranged, he enjoys the experience of responding to them because it puts him pleasurably on his toes.

The areas in which the able artist applies the principles of change include dialogue, character, the moods in the sequence of scenes, and plot. He gives thought also to the articulation of all the visual and sonant elements which may not be directly connected with advancing character and plot but which do contribute to the pace and form of the performance as a theatrical activity—and so give aid to the sensorial aliveness of the spectator. If light must follow darkness swiftly in a moment of crisis, the change is executed with precision. The sudden introduction of a new color—such as a red banner in a grey hall, or a white uniform among a group of black-robed nuns— may be just what is needed to mark the beginning of another episode. There is nothing so rightly alerting (when a scene calls for it) as the hard crack of a pistol shot, the angry clang of a bell, or an unexpected shout outside the window of a quiet room.

Actors especially need to learn the value of variety in light and sound. They must know how to use points or pools of special illumination for emphasis. They must train themselves not to pick up each other's pitch and tempo patterns. A director should cast his play as carefully as a conductor picks his voices for a choir: there must be a good balance among the sopranos, altos, tenors, and basses. Particular attention must be given to the duologues. Nothing is more disastrous to the sprightly give-and-take of a courting scene than being forced to hear it rendered by a contralto and tenor with approximately the same vocal pitch, same vocal quality, or the same inflectional and pace pattern.

As the dramatic craftsman learns to use the devices of change in the playhouse he must caution himself to handle them appropriately. Change, uncontrolled, is like dynamite; it can move what is not supposed to be moved, or it can move what is supposed to be moved too violently. When the effect of contrasts is created out of proportion to that which properly pertains to the development of the character and to the pace and the direction of the story, the playgoer may very well be jerked out of his mood of playing and not wish to return to it for the rest of the evening. What the mature dramatic artist learns by experience is to divide his working mind into two parts, one part of which he keeps on the stage, and the other by imagination in the auditorium listening to and watching his stage image.

A problem faced especially by the performer is how to show at the same time the sophisticated exterior of the character he is trying to portray and the more primitive man who is always there below the surface. The actor prepares himself to build the surface image of his part by analyzing the physical appearance, the cultured manners, and the acquired skills of the person whom it is his function to depict. This will not be very difficult.

What is considerably harder is finding the lineaments of the under image—the passionate savage, the creature whose impulses the play is essentially about—then working out a way to reveal these to the audience without destroying the surface figure. The actor will remember that the civilized man in the upper image has been bred by his social peers to hide his feelings. Yet, some-how, *the feelings below the surface must be revealed.* How? The actor will find a hint to the solution of this problem by observing the behavior of a kettle on a stove. The external appearance of the kettle is the surface image in this case; the boiling liquid inside gives the observer no indication of either its identity or the condition of its turmoil until it provides a clue. If the cover remains firmly in place, the kettle has one image only. If, how-ever, a corner of the lid rises slightly to release a puff of steam, the spectator knows at once what is inside the kettle and what it is doing there. Now not much imagination is required to con-struct a vision of the kettle's interior.

In a comparable way the actor releases, by means of apparently involuntary gestures or voice tones, hints of the primitive inside of the sophisticated shell. The surface man may be standing by a garden fence smiling as if he were completely relaxed, yet one hand held behind his back—in view of the audience but out of sight of the person the man is addressing—will be grasping a fence post as if it would crush it in anger. A faint quaver in the speaker's voice, or even an unexpected pause, may be all that is needed to suggest a state of feeling which the character, as character, had not intended to show. It is surprising how much of one's personal affection for, or antipathy to, another can be revealed in just the angle of a hand, a hesitation in a gesture, or a catch in the voice.

A potent aid to characterization is of course designed posturing and action. The actor may find of use to him the forms of the four fundamental movements of expansion and contraction, and approach and withdrawal, suggested in the chapter on Action. Every personality will use every one of these motions at some time in his appearance on the stage. But if he has an habitual tendency to use one form more than another he will be characterizing himself clearly. His posture or his action emphasizes what most reflects his nature. He will lift his head or bounce out of his chair with more spirit than he will drop his eyes toward himself or huddle himself into a chair. The aggressive man, the friendly man, or even the man filled with curiosity seems constantly to be moving forward, while the shy or fearful man, or the man who wants to have nothing to do with his fellows seems ever to be withdrawing himself, or at least just to be leaning away. The actual motion may occupy only three inches of space, but the spectator catches and grasps its meaning. The younger Willy Loman should stand much and move quickly, the older Willy should prefer sitting. The last image of Mother Courage plodding out after the Army should be that of a footsore and very bent woman.

A full use of change means more than the skillful exploiting of variations in physical stimuli. Beyond them is the intelligent interplay of ideas. The series of changes which together make action must be continuous and must move forward toward a goal. One effective means for showing the progress, or change, of impelling forces in the action is the four movements just noted, here applied to the depiction of thoughts: expanding and contracting, indicative of urges to reach out into life or to sink away from it; and approaching and withdrawing, suggestive of desires to make contact with objects and people, or to withdraw from contact into the sanctuary of oneself. The changes can be shown vividly in pantomime; they can be reflected also, as already stated, by alterations of speech tones. Sometimes just a small lifting or dropping of a hand, or a faint reaching or receding of a voice-note can imply more about the drift of a dramatic scene than fifteen minutes of explanatory dialogue.

By now it should be clear that the forms of illumination discussed in this and the preceding chapters are affected by just the same factors of contrast and change as are the forms of general excitation described in the earlier chapters. The intellectual aspects of dramatic design are based on comparisons, and comparisons are founded on a recognition of opposites in conflict: the playwright's stand *vs.* the playgoer's, a modern viewpoint *vs.* a traditional, one character's belief *vs.* another's, the individual's mind *vs.* the crowd's, a tragic perspective *vs.* a comic, hatred *vs.* compassion, cruelty *vs.* mercy, aggression *vs.* recession —there are limitless kinds. It is true that all of these differentiations occur in other literary works, such as the novel. But in the stage work the contrasts are shown more pointedly. And the changes are made more swiftly and continuously. Thus, the dramatic experience of the spectator in the playhouse is permitted no period of rest between stimulations. From first to last his responses, intellectual as well as physical, proceed, not in a gentle flow, but in forceful leaps.

To repeat: theatric art is the art of sharp changes in stimulation produced by variations of sensation, emotions and states of thought. One of the opposites may predominate, but it is always accompanied to some extent by its complement or shadow. Without the contrast for reference, no shape, quality, or condition can have a truly distinctive identity. (Compare the undifferentiated dramatic image with the piece of white-marble sculpture lighted strictly from the front with no provision for shadows to bring out the shifting planes, or with a painting rendered in nothing but green or blue.) Form needs the presence of contrast, to show itself as form.

Theatric art may be summarized then as the art of changes between opposites related by the central blood stream of the play. The effectiveness of the dramatic work depends on two things: on the strength of the contrasts and on the skill with which the proportions between them are managed.

One shift between differences of physical, mental, or emotional condition makes, as we have stated, *a change*. A sequence of such changes makes *action*.

The playwright gets at the heart of action by working on the inward thinking and feeling of the characters in his drama. So long as he can keep these turning one way, then another, his play will be bound to have action. The best device for creating the changes desired is a conflict. The resisting force of a big obstacle—commonly the counterdrive of an antagonist—will face the central character with many (dramatically valuable) difficulties. The protagonist's engagement with these, if they are well spaced, will cause a strong sense of continuing activity. For the spectator, *dramatic action is a series of changes between contrasts experienced in the pursuit of an adjustment about which the spectator is feelingly concerned.*

Among the artists who have to deal with the demands of the playgoer, the actor holds a unique place since his relationship to those who wish to be affected is at all times intimate and direct. He presents himself. There is no intermediary. He uses as his means of communication what the spectator's senses cannot possibly ignore: the actor's own wonderfully flexible body. The movements and sounds which emanate from this human instrument are capable of being inflected in an infinite number of ways in accordance with four elements of sensuous design: space, time, force, and quality.

Pantomimically, the actor uses the spatial factor in the size and the shape of his bodily movements. He lifts, he reaches, he points. He walks from place to place; he rises, sits down, lies down, and gets up again. He exploits the four "fundamental movements" referred to in Chapter III under directions of dramatic action.

Vocally, the actor employs the values of space when he shifts the pitch of his voice, and when he bends his tonal sounds into patterns of speech. He uses the spatial aspect of sound also when he makes his tones suggest motion and thereby gives the spectator a feeling of lift and fall or reaching outward toward, or retreating backward from, contact with another person. By doing this the actor reinforces the effect of the pantomime.

The time factor includes both rhythm and pace. Pantomimically and vocally these work powerfully on the senses and the mind of the spectator. On the feeling level they affect him—sometimes almost hypnotically—like the insistent beat in patterns of dance or song. On the thoughtful level they express meanings related to strain and release, restriction and expansion, and, often, the states of grief and joy.

Force includes both volume and intensity, and in pantomime and speech these are potent factors. Volume is size, intensity is inner strength which may or may not take the form of size. A very small gesture or an almost inaudible stage whisper, for instance, may provide on occasion the little sting which begins a revolution or sets a whole army into motion.

Quality covers impressions of sensuality or imperviousness, softness or hardness, tenderness or brutality. This factor works in physical movements and in speech sounds both sensuously and intellectually. It, like the other factors of design, is capable of limitless variety.

Each of the elements referred to—space, time, force, and quality—stands, in a way, for a whole dimension of expressiveness. All the shades and turns of change are the actor's to reveal. And he can indicate them fully—not just through the use of the word forms which the playwright has set down in his lettered script, but also through all those motions and sounds which are implied but not stated between the lines of the script.

The playwright's task is to manage his blocks and releases so that they will have the right degree of strength and the proper amount of speed to create the emotional warmth he wishes to obtain for each particular situation. How successful he will be depends on his sense of proportions. He must have, first, a good eye for the drive he is building up behind each block. If a character's want to reach a goal is overpowering, the block that restrains it must be equal to its force, or the drive will simply override it. If the urge is too small, the block which is placed in its path may seem ridiculous, and the feeling that is held back by the block will appear to be pitiful or even laughable, rather than serious.

Likewise, the emotional explosion itself must be handled with skill. If, to the sudden removal of a big block, the response of the person most involved turns out to be unequal to what was promised by all the build-up, the effect on the audience will be unsatisfactory. Equally disappointing will be a contrived outburst which springs from a situation in which the drive was great but the block was small, and the removal of this really deserved no strong expression of feeling at all!

There are several other points in the creation of the dramatic feelings that the author and his fellow playmakers should keep in mind. One is the preparation for the critical moment. The more a desire has had a chance to cumulate in flow, or on the other hand to gather up behind an impediment, the more powerful will tend to be the emotional "bang" that follows the sudden thwarting or emancipation. And at the same time, the more violent will likely be the action which expresses that feeling. The boy who has been courting a girl for a long time may now, tonight, expect her to accept his proposal. But for some reason she says "no." The result may be his going out to get drunk. Perhaps, if the flow of his previous feeling was very strong and her refusal now really hits him hard, he will drive away in his car and plunge it off a cliff. Under opposite circumstances, a boy who has greatly desired a girl for several months and does not now expect a favorable response from her, gets a "yes!" His reaction may be a delighted whoop or a happy jig. Or he may go down to the nearest drugstore and treat himself to the biggest strawberry sundae that he can obtain there!

One of the most potent causes, both of the pleasant and unpleasant feelings and of the emotions, is the opposition of two more basic feelings, one of which serves in effect as a holding force on the other. If one has pleasure in a beautiful evening but is held back from going out into it by a cold, one will have a feeling of impatience. If one is attracted to a lovely face but is at the same time repelled by a blemish on it, one will have another kind of unpleasant feeling. A person moved by his love of a child and his hatred of a sudden display of bad manners by that child may get quite angry.

Quite paradoxically, some oppositions cause desirable feelings. This is especially true in those cases where a temporary frustration whets the appetite for a joyous fulfillment later on. A restraint which prevents the person from discharging all at once his urge to unite himself with the object of his desire tends to raise feelings of longing, together with a hope, an anticipation, which is in part at least pleasant. It is commonplace that a wise woman who wishes to retain the affection of her husband uses restraint; she never gives him all of herself at one time. She yields just enough to him to feed his pleasurable feelings, but she never lets him have enough of her to satiate him, for if she did, love would turn to dull contentment. Contentment breeds no desirable emotion. It is mere neutrality. If, however, the restraint is too long sustained, the affection is apt to turn into impatience or even aversion.

Another important point for one to remember always is that sudden shifts of thought can cause emotion just like changes of action. Regard the little girl who has been sent inside the house because of bad weather and then one morning sees the sun. She is all set to run out to play when her mother informs her that because of her cold she must stay in another day. Physically, the condition of the little girl has not changed. Mentally, however, a whole group of lovely images of her outdoors has been snatched from her mind. The result is likely to be a tantrum.

Effects of tragedy and comedy must be handled discreetly by the playwright. The treatment of pain on the stage is pleasurable or distasteful to an audience in accordance with the way it is managed. Pain, when its origin and reason for being are clearly understood by the audience, and when its duration is definitely limited, may be quite stimulating. If the experience of hurt gets out of control, however—if the kind of distress in which the spectator is asked by imagination to participate is excessive, unduly mysterious, and overprolonged—it may cause a feeling of revulsion. The audience seldom wants to be left in a state of real depression at the end of the evening. It can take a considerable dose of tragedy if the playwright follows it with at least a little relief at the end. This may take the form of a change of fortune or a "revelation"—a flash of understanding—which makes the pain experienced seem to have a kind of human meaningfulness transcending the hurt of the episode enacted.

Comic effects also have to be handled with care. The amusing comments which take their nourishment out of another person's discomfort have to be executed with real skill or they will turn back in a curve to cut the author more than his subject. The dramatist who deals with the type of comedy which contains a sting usually safeguards himself by employing enough distortion to create an effect of cartooning. The figures on the stage, their actions and their words, are formed enough like the human beings they are lampooning to make the point of satire clear, yet they are allowed to be enough unlike to let the audience's feeling of fair play remain unchallenged. No actual blood is allowed to flow.

It is very important for the dramatist to remember at all times Max Eastman's warning that the comic artist must be sure that his respondent is in a condition of fun before he begins to play tricks on him. At the end of a comical experience the spectator wants to feel himself in a state of grace. The author and the actor must work in partnership to achieve the desired effect. This is especially true in the creation of those comic scenes in which the emphasis is directed more toward lively action than to intellectual smartness. Always, the condition of "being in fun" has importance.

It may be of help to the comic playwright to remind himself frequently of the two principal causes of laughter: (a) whatever brings about a sudden access to a new insight (a special recognition of the essential relationship of opposites—pride and debasement, anticipation and frustration, harmony and incongruity, the patch on the dress pants); (b) whatever brings about a sudden feeling of lively well-being. Above all things the author must remember that the effect of value is that which is produced in the spectator, not in himself. The comic writer, more than anyone else in the theatre, has to be fundamentally a man of generous good will—toward his spectator if not toward his subject.

Creating the kind of character which will appeal to a playgoer's wish for identification requires a nice sense of balance between exaggeration and verisimilitude. Clearly, the figure on stage must be larger than life; he must excel in certain selected qualities which the playgoer finds interesting and compelling; otherwise the playgoer would not take the trouble to go to the playhouse to observe him. There are plenty of ordinary life-sized people around one's home or office all too available for view every hour of the day. At the same time, the stage figure cannot be too big, too perfect, or he will not seem convincing; the playgoer will feel no impulse to unite his body or mind with him. He may even resent him. The playgoer will give himself more readily to a wonderfully brave character if this man shows a little fear of dogs, perhaps, or if a handsome woman scares him to death. The physically powerful figure has to favor a wrist weakened by an old accident. The sharp mathematician complains about the trouble he has in working out his income tax. The saintly individual has a temper.

The able general, the dedicated leader of government, the beloved rebel must never look like a matinee idol. George Washington, who biographers tell us was actually a very human person, has suffered throughout our history from being too handsome. He has become much more likable—much more the kind of personality with whose astounding courage we would like to unite our own aspirations—since we have learned that he had big awkward hands, was subject to colds, and had dreadful trouble with his teeth.

Likewise we are attracted to people of faith—and through them to the quality of those institutions that compel their loyalty—when we know that they occasionally are plagued by doubts. The doubts make them human like the rest of us, and thus the doubts provide us with a kind of steppingstone into the greater conviction the dramatic figures represent.

Plays about rascals require a similar kind of shading, only reversed. The blackest villain becomes even more inky when he helps a blind man cross the street. The playgoer wants to feel himself entering the mind of both his protagonists and antagonists, but only when he senses that they are human enough to be at the same time commanding figures, and lifelike individuals, will he feel free to project himself into them.

Since all dramatic form grows out of human nature, and human nature is the basic ingredient of dramatic composition, the dramatist is wise to pick the dominant character for a play with special thought for his power to motivate it. This means that the character should be first of all a man or a woman capable of change. He should not be so unemotional as not to care about change, nor too stupid to see a need for change, nor so stolid as to resist acting out a change if one seemed advisable.

Having selected such an individual, the dramatist will put him into a condition ripe for a change: (a) a little too high, or too low, in fortune, for it to seem right—according to the spectator's code of poetic justice—for him to maintain that position indefinitely; (b) a little too peaceful, or too happily active, for his condition to seem quite natural in this unstable world. Assuming that the protagonist regards himself to be on balance, the playwright will have to push him off it by some thrust from his environment. Since this environment is in effect everything that is not one's essential self, the challenging force may be, as we have seen, an action of the physical world—like a stirring up of the sea, a flood, or a disease—or, more likely, a willful deed by another man, or even a disturbing obsession from another side of the protagonist himself.

Now, presumably, the protagonist will attempt to regain his poise—or strive for a new one. His effort to do this will constitute the drama. The more extreme the difference between the height from which he drops, the peacefulness from which he is jolted, and the turmoil toward which he is impelled, the more striking (dramatic) will seem to be the result.

Young writers often have a lot of trouble with the problems of convincing motivation. When asked just what a certain stage personality *wants*, and what in the light of this want he is *trying to do*, the author is apt to reply frankly, "I don't know," then to inquire naïvely, "but does that matter?" The assumption seems to be that an audience which gets plenty of dialogue and interesting movement should not care where the action is going. The assumption is false, of course. It violates the second premise stated at the very beginning of this book, that is, that the spectator *does want to understand what is going on!*

More often the young writer attempts to hide his confusion by trying to make a virtue of freedom from control. "I don't want to have my character's behavior be too explicit," he remarks. "I want to let the audience make up its own mind about him." The kindest reply that one can give to an author making this kind of dramaturgical declaration is to call his attention to the related art of photography. In it there are two ways to create a soft-focus picture. One way to get a misty portrait of a pretty girl is simply to turn the lens of the camera a little out of focus. The result is an achievement of fuzzy outlines. But they are not satisfying. The person who looks at the portrait feels an impulse to blink to clear his sight. "Where are her eyes?" he will say. "I want to see her eyes!" If he cannot find them he is likely to be irritated instead of pleased; he will feel that the photographer has done his work carelessly. The other, the legitimate way to get the misty effect, is to use a genuine soft-focus lens, and with this to focus on the subject just as carefully as one would with a regular lens. The product now is a portrait which combines definition with softness. The observer sees a picture in which the lovely subject has clear, seeing eyes, affected however by a faintly dewy quality which accentuates their mysteriousness.

About the handling of the so-called "difficult" plays, such as Harold Pinter's, it is very fashionable in certain playmaking circles today to refer to them as "great" while insisting that they are intended to be "effect pieces" only, and so do not contain any intellectual meaning. The term that is commonly used is "irrational." There seems to be a feeling that any director or actor who seeks for a meaning in these works is actually being false to the purpose of Pinter's original intent. This seems to me a strange attitude. Does it reveal on the part of the commentator a wishful desire to hide a breakdown in his perspicacity? I am tempted to believe it does. Pinter (to continue the example) is quite clearly striving to detach himself from the more easily verbalized theatrical clichés. But to insist that he stops there is, I think, unfair. If one is willing to dig a little one can find a very possible meaning in a world of aggressive and passive mask-wearers and the effects they produce on the insecure individuals who are forced to confront them. The pathetic Davies in *The Caretaker* tries desperately to keep his mask on and fails. The Matchseller in *A Slight Ache* gains something by doing nothing more than assuming the role of pure presence. All the characters in *The Homecoming* (pre-eminently Teddy and Ruth) shift their masks with surprising results.

It is true that the author of these particular plays has declared somewhere that he himself does not know what they mean. This is a brave statement that should not be taken too seriously; dramatists are notoriously inarticulate when they attempt to explain their intuitively-arrived-at theatrical visions. One needs only to recall the sputtering declarations of Anton Chekov and our own Edward Albee. An intelligent spectator enjoys using his mind to hunt around for the core of a dramatic idea. What he thoroughly dislikes is being told by a director, a critic, or the author himself that there actually was no idea there to begin with—or that the observer has to supply the idea!

A wise author achieves a right effect of poetic mistiness in drama by never letting himself have any doubt as to what exists behind the veil. Thus the audience, trusting the integrity of the playwright, faces enjoyably the challenge of trying to solve a riddle to which he knows that there *is* an answer if he would just look hard enough. Says T. S. Eliot in *Selected Essays*: "The suggestiveness of true poetry . . . is the aura round a bright clear centre. You cannot have the aura alone." He might well have said the same thing about drama. The suggestive aura of a play, just like a poem, must pivot on a point. There is no successful suggestion without the point.

Emotional warmth in a play springs from a premise that there is at least some value in the act of cherishing an object. Whatever that thing is derives its importance from being connected with pulsing, breathing human nature. So humanity is the base of all; if it is eliminated, theatre has small reason for being.

With respect to that human ingredient the dramatist must be at the same time a defender and a critic. First of all he is a lover. Whatever attack on his subject he chooses to take, he begins with compassion. If his attitude is romantic, he is an idealist. If he is a tragedian or a comic, he is likewise an idealist; pain and foolishness are states of being that he contrasts with a norm which he assumes the spectator accepts as a premise. Even the bitterest of true satirists holds humanity as *capable* of perfection, as *worthy* of being seen in that condition of grace; otherwise his criticism, without a contrary reference, will have no bite at all. Satire without affection is peevishness only.

Says the dramatist William Inge: "A man writes out of himself, out of his own roots, out of his own experience." Says Bernard Shaw: "The man who writes about himself and his own time is the only man who writes about all people and all time." The most important facts of man viewed as individual or as mass are his ceaseless desires to live, to know and to achieve.

Common sense as well as tradition insists that a dramatic story shall be set up with a firm beginning and a firm ending. Dramatic heat breeds in compression. The more the ending pushes back on the beginning—or the closer the beginning approaches the ending—the more forceful is the sense of dilemma which the compression engenders. Consequently, the emotions are more violent in everyone concerned. As much as the protagonist might wish that he could extend the period of his working for achievement, he finds that he cannot. He must make his decision regarding his career, say, before his lawyer calls at 4:00 o'clock tomorrow; or he must win his young lady's consent before she leaves on the plane at 3:00 this afternoon; or he must find a way to repair a piece of equipment swiftly in order to prevent the fatal explosion that threatens now at any minute. This concentration is what makes theatrical excitement.

The fundamental responsibility for injecting into a play those factors which will satisfy a spectator's desire for a sense of achievement (sentimental or intellectual) is the playwright's. Nevertheless, the actor can and must make a sizable contribution in the way he translates the author's concepts into the visible and audible figures that are related to the search. The actor builds by sensuous means the image of a *self* with which the spectator can deal by imagination in his effort to feel identity. Or, the actor constructs a figure (by the same means) with which the spectator can react in a contrary way and, by doing so, find his place in an opposing self. There is nothing that serves more potently to make a person define his own attitudes than a clearly pointed challenge.

This does not mean that an actor has to channel his efforts into the designing of a sharply marked white or black character. Often the more shaded, devious, or mobile a stage personality is the more compelling he becomes. The spectator, self-imaged in the purposeful adventure of finding a stance with regard to the forces which surround him, likes to see his search complicated by many twists of sense and thought. The complications enlarge the feeling of experience. However, generally speaking, he likes to arrive in the end at a well-focused identity.

The actor can help the spectator's attainment of a feeling of power by clarifying his character's behavior with respect to motives and drives. At the close of the play the spectator should feel fulfilled. If what he gets is a sense of failure, it should possess a feeling of meaningfulness so that there will be no sense of waste; what the protagonist loses in fortune or comfort he gets, by way of compensation, in clarity of insight. If the spectator has been deliberately prevented from a personal participation in the action, he should be able to feel at the end at least the satisfaction of an Olympian perspective on the foregoing dramatic events. As we have suggested elsewhere, one of the finest attainments a spectator can have in the theatre is the sense of philosophical understanding.

Living reality in art consists not in setting any fixed patterns of plotting but in the selection of just a few vigorous elements of human action and feeling, in assembling these for an increased sense of vitality—and doing it all in such a way as to make the spectator feel that during the period of his watching he is, in effect, ordering certain disparate parts of his own life. His experience of playgoing then provides him with two wonderful sensations at the same time: feeling invigorated and feeling integrated.

SELECTED BIBLIOGRAPHY

ARTAUD, ANTONIN. *The Theatre and Its Double*. New York: Grove
Press, 1958.
This book has exerted a strong influence on the substance and
form of the theatre of revolt in Europe and America, particularly the Theatre of Cruelty.

BERNE, ERIC. *Games People Play*. New York: Grove Press, 1964.
A psychiatrist looks at the way in which many of man's transactions are effected through the means of games.

BRUSTEIN, ROBERT S. *Theatre of Revolt: An Approach to the
Modern Drama*. Boston: Little, Brown, 1964.
Studies in the nonconformist authors from Ibsen to Genet.

CAILLOIS, ROGER. *Man, Play and Games*. Translated from the
French by Meyer Borash. New York: Free Press of Glencoe,
Inc., 1961.
A provocative essay on the human propensity to engage in
games.

CLARK, BARRETT H. *European Theories of the Drama*, with a sup-
plement on the American drama. Newly revised by Henry
Popkin. New York: Crown Publishers, 1965.
An anthology of dramatic criticism from Aristotle to Duer-
renmatt in Europe, and from Brander Matthews to Eric
Bentley in the United States, in selected texts with commen-
taries.

DOWNER, ALAN S. *Fifty Years of American Drama, 1900–1950*.
Chicago: Regnery, 1951.
A short but useful critical guide to the principal American
plays of the first half of the century, so arranged as to group
together the theatrical, romantic, realistic, folk, and experi-
mental works; with a special chapter on comedy.

EDMAN, IRWIN. *The World, the Arts and the Artist*. New York:
W. W. Norton and Company, 1939.
A perceptive and invigorating book of essays on the nature
and uses of the arts by one of America's leading philosophers in
esthetics.

EISLER, ROBERT. *Man into Wolf*. London: Rutledge and Paul,
1951.

In a long essay and a number of supplementary notes Eisler speculates on the origins of man's fascination in actions of violence and cruelty.

HUIZINGA, J. *Homo Ludens: A Study of the Play Element in Culture.* New York: Roy Publishers, 1950.

The author, an eminent historian, maintains that the story of the human race would have been very different from what it is if man had not been by nature from the beginning fundamentally playful.

JONES, ROBERT E. *The Dramatic Imagination.* New York: Theatre Arts Books, 1941.

A short statement of his beliefs as an artist written from the heart of a man who in his day was the pre-eminent designer in the American theatre.

KERR, WALTER. *How Not to Write a Play.* New York: Simon and Schuster, 1955.

Probably the best guide to playwriting that was ever composed.

KERR, WALTER. *Tragedy and Comedy.* New York: Simon and Schuster, 1967.

A brilliant exploration of the nature of tragedy viewed as light and of comedy seen as its contrasting and complementary shadow. Mr. Kerry examines the reason for the present lack of truly vigorous plays in both fields.

LORENZ, KONRAD. *On Aggression.* New York: Harcourt, Brace and World, Inc., 1963.

An examination of the fundamental aggressive impulse in animals and in people that breeds their competitive actions and their unending struggle with others of their kind.

MAY, ROLLO. *Man's Search for Himself.* New York: W. W. Norton and Company, 1953.

A psychologist investigates the kinds of hunger that make people restless and suggests how, with guidance, they overcome them. There is much in the book that can be applied to the playgoer's search for satisfaction in the theatre.

MITCHELL, ELMER D., and Bernard S. Mason. *The Theory of Play.* New York: A. A. Barnes and Company, 1948.

A classic treatise.

PAULHAN, FREDRIC. *The Laws of Feeling.* New York: Harcourt, Brace and Company, 1930.

The author is an authority in this field. What he states about feeling clarifies the motivations of dramatic action.

SELDEN, SAMUEL. *Man in His Theatre*. Chapel Hill: The University of North Carolina Press, 1957.
An examination of the origins of drama with suggestions on how some of the early conventions are applicable today.

SELDEN, SAMUEL. *The Stage in Action*. A reprint. Carbondale: Southern Illinois University Press, 1967.
The interrelationship of the arts of acting, dancing, music, and painting, and how they continue to depend fruitfully on each other with regard to form and motive.

SINNOTT, EDMOND. *Cell and Psyche: The Biology of Purpose*. Chapel Hill: The University of North Carolina Press, 1950.
A leading scientist in the field of both animal and human life shows how the roots of man's efforts to progress and better himself started on the lowest step of his evolution.

SZASZ, THOMAS STEPHEN. *Pain and Pleasure: A Study of Bodily Feelings*. New York: Basic Books, 1957.
Another revealing work in the field of feelings.

YOUNG, PAUL THOMAS. *Emotions in Man and Animals*. New York: John Wiley and Sons, 1943.
Still another standard work on feelings.